SOUTHERN QUILTS

SOUTHERN QUILTS

Surviving Relics of
THE CIVIL WAR

Bets Ramsey and Merikay Waldvogel

RUTLEDGE HILL PRESS®

NASHVILLE, TENNESSEE

Published by Rutledge Hill Press®, 211 Seventh Avenue North, Nashville, Tennessee 37219.
Distributed in Canada by H. B. Fenn & Company, Ltd., 34 Nixon Road, Bolton, Ontario L7E 1W2.
Distributed in Australia by The Five Mile Press Pty. Ltd., 22 Summit Road, Noble Park, Victoria 3174.
Distributed in New Zealand by Tandem Press, 2 Rugby Road, Birkenhead, Auckland 10.
Distributed in the United Kingdom by Verulam Publishing, Ltd., 152a Park Street Lane, Park Street,
  St. Albans, Hertfordshire AL2 2AU.

Cover, page design, and typesetting by Harriette Bateman

Library of Congress Cataloging-in-Publication Data

Ramsey, Bets, 1923–
    Southern quilts: surviving relics of the Civil War / Bets Ramsey and Merikay Waldvogel.
        p.   cm.
    Includes Index.
    ISBN 1-55853-598-5 (pb)
    1. Quilts—Southern States—History—19th century. I. Waldvogel. Merikay, 1947–   .   II. Title
NK9112.R373   1998
746.46'0975'09034—dc21   98–2846
                                                                          CIP

Printed in Singapore
1 2 3 4 5 6 7 8 9—00 99 98

CONTENTS

REFACE

IT HAS OFTEN been said, "If only these quilts could talk, could tell us their stories, what a lot we would learn!" Even without a verbal language there are ways to unlock some of the secrets and add to the family lore which often accompanies old quilts. By interpreting various characteristics a definite profile emerges to capture something of a quilt's life story. The fabric, pattern, technique, and general appearance provide information about the age, styles, traditions, economic factors, quality of life, and ability of the maker. This technical examination substantiates, or possibly negates, the oral account provided by the quilt's caretaker.

We have made a concerted effort to verify the stories of these survivors of the Civil War period, but if, in the telling, there has been some embellishment, we beg your indulgence. Many of the quilts have had harrowing adventures and troublesome existences, reminding us of a time when our nation experienced one of the most critical periods in its history.

— BETS RAMSEY AND MERIKAY WALDVOGEL

CIVIL WAR TIME LINE

1860

November 6: Following Abraham Lincoln's election as U.S. president, several slave-holding states call conventions to consider secession.

December 20: South Carolina secedes.

1861

January 9: Mississippi secedes, followed by Florida (Jan. 10), Alabama (Jan. 11), Georgia (Jan. 19), and Louisiana (Jan. 26).

January 29: Kansas is admitted to the Union.

February 4: Convention of seceded states opens in Montgomery, Ala. Within days delegates frame the Constitution of the Confederate States of America and elect Jefferson Davis president. Shortly thereafter, most federal property in the Southern states is seized.

February 18: Davis is inaugurated in Montgomery.

March 4: Lincoln is inaugurated as the sixteenth president of the United States.

April 12–13: Confederate forces bombard and capture Fort Sumter at Charleston, S.C. Lincoln calls for 75,000 volunteers to quell the insurrection.

April 17: Virginia secedes, followed by Arkansas (May 6), North Carolina (May 20), and Tennessee (June 8).

July 21: First battle of Bull Run at Manassas, Va. The Confederates score a decisive tactical victory.

July 27: George B. McClellan is named commander of Union armies.

July–November: The Union navy blockades Southern ports.

1862

February 6–16: Northern victories in Tennessee at Forts Henry and Donelson. On February 25 Nashville becomes the first Confederate state capital to fall to Union forces.

March 8: The CSS *Virginia*, the first ironclad ship of the war, attacks Union vessels blockading Hampton Roads, Va. It sinks two ships, drives another aground, and the next day battles the Union ironclad *Monitor* to a draw.

April 5: The Peninsula campaign begins as Union forces approach Yorktown, Va.

April 6–7: Battle of Shiloh in West Tennessee. Casualties are staggering on both sides (23,700 total), but the Union victory dooms the Confederates in the West.

April 16: The Confederacy enacts conscription.

April 25: New Orleans falls to the Union navy.

May 31–June 1: Battle of Seven Pines (Fair Oaks), Va. Each side sends nearly 42,000 troops onto the field, but the battle is indecisive. The Confederate commander, Joseph E. Johnston is wounded; he is replaced by Robert E. Lee.

June 25–July 1: The Seven Days' battles

dramatically reverse the course of the war in Virginia. McClellan's army is driven off the peninsula.

August 29–30: Second battle of Bull Run. Lee defeats a Union army under John Pope, and the Southern victory removes all Federal forces from Virginia.

September 4: The Army of Northern Virginia begins the first invasion of the North.

September 15: Thomas J. "Stonewall" Jackson captures Harpers Ferry, Va.

September 17: Battle of Antietam, Md. On the bloodiest single day in American history, casualties total 23,000.

November 7: Ambrose E. Burnside takes over the Army of the Potomac after McClellan is relieved of command.

December 13: Battle of Fredericksburg, Va. Federal casualties exceed 12,000 in the South's most one-sided victory of the war.

December 31–January 2: Battle of Stones River, near Murfreesboro, Tenn. A tactical stalemate, but Southern forces retreat to Chattanooga.

1863

January 1: Lincoln issues the Emancipation Proclamation, freeing all slaves in "rebellious sections" of the country.

January 25: Burnside is relieved of command; he is replaced by Joseph E. Hooker.

March: The Union's first Conscription Act is enacted. Viewed as unfair to the poor, the legislation results in rioting in working-class sections of New York City.

May 3–4: Battle of Chancellorsville, Va. Lee defeats Hooker although outnumbered almost two to one.

May 10: "Stonewall" Jackson dies after being mistakenly shot by his own troops at Chancellorsville.

May 19: The siege of Vicksburg, Miss., begins.

May 22: The first all-volunteer African-American regiment raised in the North, the Fifty-fourth Massachusetts Volunteer Infantry, is mustered into Federal service.

June 20: West Virginia is admitted to the Union. The new state is comprised of Virginia's mountainous western counties, whose residents opted not to secede from the United States.

June 28: Hooker is relieved of command; he is replaced by George Gordon Meade.

July 1–3: Battle of Gettysburg, Pa. Lee's invasion is blunted as he loses a third of his army, relinquishes the field, and retreats back to Virginia.

July 4: Vicksburg, Miss., surrenders after a thirty-seven-day siege. The Union victories at Gettysburg and Vicksburg mark the military turning point of the war.

September 19–20: Battle of Chickamauga, Ga. After pushing the Confederates from Chattanooga, William S. Rosecrans's army is mauled by Southern troops in north Georgia and forced to retreat.

November 19: Lincoln delivers the Gettysburg Address at the commemoration of the National Soldiers' Cemetery near the battlefield.

November 23–25: Battle of Chattanooga. To break the month-long siege, Union forces attack the surrounding heights and drive the Southerners into north Georgia.

November 14–December: Longstreet lays siege to Knoxville, Tennessee, but withdraws after learning of Bragg's defeat at Chattanooga.

1864

March: Grant is given command of all Union armies.

May-June: Lee attacks Grant at the Wilderness, Va. (May 5–7). Grant pursues Lee and both suffer staggering losses at Spotsylvania (May 7–19) and Cold Harbor, Va. (June 1–3). Lee's army never recovers from the continual attacks and falls under siege at Petersburg.

May 6: Sherman begins the Atlanta campaign.

July: To relieve the siege of Petersburg, Confederate Gen. Jubal Early threatens to attack the Northern capital, coming within five miles of Washington, D.C. He is pushed back to Virginia after the battle of Monocacy, Md. (July 9).

August 2-23: Adm. David Farragut's fleet is pounded by Southern forts as it enters Mobile Bay on August 5 but forces Confederate naval units to surrender, closing the bay. The city, however, remains in Southern hands.

August 7: Philip Sheridan begins a campaign in the Shenandoah Valley to eliminate the valley as the breadbasket of the Confederacy and its use as an invasion corridor.

September 2: After more than three months of maneuvering and fighting, Union Gen. William T. Sherman takes possession of Atlanta.

September 19: Sheridan defeats Early at the third battle of Winchester, Va. Afterward, the Confederacy abandons the Shenandoah Valley.

November: Lincoln is re-elected president of the United States.

November-December: Sherman's March to the Sea. Federal soldiers devastate much of Georgia's midsection along a 250-mile line of march from Atlanta to Savannah.

November 30: Battle of Franklin, Tenn.

John B. Hood loses a third of the Army of Tennessee and six generals; the Federals withdraw to Nashville.

December 15–16: The Confederate Army of Tennessee is destroyed at the battle of Nashville, ultimately ending the war in the West.

December 22: Sherman occupies Savannah.

1865

January 31: The Thirteenth Amendment, abolishing slavery, is passed by Congress and sent to the states for ratification.

February 17: Sherman occupies Columbia, S.C. Charleston is evacuated and the next day is occupied by Union troops.

March 4: Lincoln's second inauguration.

March 25–April 1: Lee tries to break out of Petersburg and then falls back after failing to breach the Federal lines.

April 2: Jefferson Davis and his cabinet flee south. Lee retreats along the Appomattox River.

April 3: Richmond falls and is immediately occupied by Northern troops.

April 9: Lee surrenders to Grant at Appomattox Court House, Va.

April 14: Lincoln is assassinated by John Wilkes Booth and dies the next day.

April 26: Johnston surrenders the battered Army of Tennessee to Sherman.

May 12: The last official battle of the Civil War ends in a Confederate victory at Palmito Ranch, Texas.

June 23: The last Confederate army surrenders.

December 18: The Thirteenth Amendment, abolishing slavery, is ratified.

Acknowledgments

WE ARE INDEBTED to many people for their assistance in the preparation of this book. We are especially grateful to the individuals and museums whose quilts appear on these pages for their help in gathering information. Larry Stone, John Mitchell, and Rutledge Hill Press have been our strong supporters throughout this project. As always, we enjoyed our own collaboration. Our thanks go to the following individuals and institutions.

Gail A. Trechsel
Melissa B. Falkner
Robert and Helen Cargo
The Birmingham Museum of Art
Chattanooga-Hamilton County
  Bicentennial Library
Bettye Broyles
Tennessee State Museum
James A. Hoobler
Sheila Morris Green
Stephen Cox
June Dorman
Jerry Desmond
Evelyn Metzger
Susan Church
Thomas Cartwright
The Carter House Association, Inc.
Yale University Press
North Carolina Quilt Project
Ellen Eames

Ruth Roberson
Erma Kirkpatrick
Sarah Elizabeth Abernathy
Missouri Historical Society
Jerry Ledbetter
Suellen Meyer
Cuesta Benberry
Virginia F. Gilman
John-Paul Richiuso
Tennessee State Library & Archives
McMinn County Living Heritage Museum
Atlanta History Center
Betsy Weyburn
Polly Boggess
Diana Stimson Webb
Old Capitol Museum of Mississippi
  History
Mary Lorenz
Kentucky Quilt Project
Shelly Zegart

Hardin Pettit
Kit Jeans Mounger
Jonesborough Visitors Center Museum
Diane Maillet
Jeanne Gilmore Webb
Hunter Museum of American Art
Ellen Simac
Mary Heiskell Wasson
Ann S. Davis
McMinn County Living Heritage Museum
McMinn County Historical Society
Gay McNemer
Charla Honea
The Museum of Texas Tech University
Howard Michael Madaus
Malcolm Rogers
Nancy Hornback
Betty Mills
Madge Robb
Sharon Newman
East Tennessee Historical Society
Calvin M. McClung Historical Collection,
   Knox County Public Library
Steve Cotham
Special Collections, Hodges Library at the
   University of Tennessee-Knoxville
Dorothy Cozart

Kansas State Historical Society
Barbara Brackman
William S. Scott
Bryding Adams
Ella Ree Bounds
James Bell
Larry Bounds
John and Abby Graber
Jean Loken
Jean Hatch
Carroll Reece Museum, East Tennessee
   State University
Blair White
Maryanna Smith Huff
Betty McDowell
Judy Elwood
Emeline Prince Gist
Julie Silber
Pat Ferraro
Hearts and Hands Media Arts
Marilyn DeMarcus Harmon
Ethel Duff
Kathryn Susong Neas
Judith Trager
Ken Sanville
Guy Hubbs

If we have neglected to record other names that should appear here, we are no less grateful and, indeed, offer our thanks.

SOUTHERN QUILTS

A Quilter Writes About the Civil War's Causes

The following was excerpted from the diary of Annie B. Darden, a housewife who lived with her husband and five children on a small farm in Buckhorn, Hertford County, North Carolina, just south of the Virginia border.

MARCH 4. There has been no sunshine today. The heavens seem to be hung with darkness, over our nation's wrongs. Yes today, I fear, will seal the sad, sad fate of our country's history, for this is the day for the inauguration of a President. That will cause a dissolution of our Union; and we know not what other ill will follow. We can only look to Him whose power alone sways heaven & earth. But the die is cast; our Star spangled banner will wave no more over us as a free united & happy people. The mad fanatics of the North seem bent on the destruction of the South. They have been throwing fire brands in our midst for years, secretly. Now they have come out with a black republican President resolved to carry out their wicked designs at the risk of life, happiness & virtue. My Lord subdue the foul spirits & save us as a people from war & blood shed. The South has borne the insults of the North too long. Bur forbearance has ceased & now the crisis has arrived; some are standing idle instead of presenting one unbroken front. We are divided among ourselves; some noble States have seceded while others are quietly submitting to the Enemy & talking about Union when there is NONE. The SAD TRUTH, the UNION is gone, and the tie that bound us is broken. The golden links have been rudely severed by the politicians & the abolitionists of the North. Instead of peace, now, we hear rumors of war & division, & today . . .

MARCH 19. I have finished all the squares for my quilt. I think I shall call it a DISUNION QUILT as it will be made different from any I ever saw.

UNITED WE STAND, DIVIDED WE FALL

THE FIRST HALF of the nineteenth century saw the United States of America striving to carve its own niche among the nations of the world. With the defeat of the British in the War of 1812, the central government feared foreign enemies less than it did the widening divisions among the country's diverse population. Sectional differences between the North and South—spawned by a complex mixture of social, economic, and political factors—grew stronger with each passing year, and the lofty ideals espoused by the founding fathers increasingly seemed beyond the reach of the fledgling nation.

In the North, industrial growth began to overshadow agricultural endeavors, attracting capital as well as thousands of immigrant workers who would soon become citizens. In the South, there was little industrial development, hence fewer settlers, and the region continued to be almost solely dependent on a cotton-based agricultural economy. Cotton farming was very labor-intensive, thus the "peculiar institution" of slavery remained a part of life on some Southern farms and plantations for years. It is interesting to note that the cotton gin, the device that made cotton production economically viable—and thereby increased the need for large numbers of low-cost hand laborers—was invented by a Northerner, Eli Whitney.

Sectional hostilities increased markedly following the Missouri Compromise of 1820, which was intended to resolve the question of whether to allow or prohibit slavery in America's resource-rich western territories. This territorial issue perhaps most clearly delineated the differences between the two factions. Although many Southerners believed that slavery was an anachronism in an enlightened society, they feared that banning the practice in the West ultimately would undermine the South's economy and weaken its representation in the U.S. Congress.

Also key to the sectional dispute was a series of import tariffs imposed by Congress that were designed to force Southern states to buy manufactured items from their Northern neighbors rather than from England and France, where goods were cheaper and more plentiful. The tariffs, called "protective" in the North and "punitive" in the South, angered Southerners, many of whom had business ties with European countries. In fact, European mills were purchasing Southern cotton at such a high rate that sales totaled more than half of all American exports prior to 1860.

Pointing out that the U.S. Constitution allowed states the right to ignore (or "nullify") a federal law, the South Carolina legislature in November 1832 passed an Ordinance of Nullification, refusing to collect the tariff and threatening to withdraw from the Union. Congress responded to the talks of secession by revising the tariff in February 1833, but the incident caused Southern leaders to speak out more ardently for the rights of states to govern themselves.

The rise of abolitionist sentiment in the North during the 1830s further exacerbated problems between the North and South. For years, Congress had attempted to maintain a balance of political power by simultaneously admitting slave and free states to the Union. Since cotton—and thus slavery—was not adaptable to the western territories, many Southerners felt those regions eventually would be admitted as free states, and as a result, advocated the annexation of Texas, which they expected would be admitted as a slave state. A slave uprising led by Nat Turner in Virginia in 1831, which resulted in the deaths of fifty-five whites and sixteen blacks, further divided the factions and led to a series of more stringent slave laws in the South.

The Compromise of 1850 was enacted primarily to prevent the slavery issue from causing dissolution of the Union. Its provisions included the admission of California as a free state and enactment of a new fugitive slave law requiring Northerners to return escaped slaves to their owners. While the latter provision was intended to cool Southern ire, Northern states passed legislation superceding the federal measure, and escaped slaves were seldom returned. Further, the law became a symbol of resistance to both pro- and antislavery groups, and deepened the chasm between the regions.

From 1837 to 1860, the United States elected eight presidents, but sectional animosities were so strong that none served more than a single term. The campaign rhetoric of 1860 was especially strident as vocal abolitionists in the North claimed the moral high ground and sought to make slavery the focal point of the presidential election. By forcing each candidate to take a stand on slavery, they polarized the national debate.

Abolitionists comprised less than 3 percent of the population at large, but they were welcomed by the Republican Party, which added an anti-slavery plank to its platform. The Republicans nominated Abraham Lincoln, one of Illinois's most competent attorneys, as their presidential candidate. Lincoln, who had voiced his opposition to the institution of slavery more than a decade earlier as a Whig Congressman and during an unsuccessful bid for the Senate, emerged victorious in the national election in November 1860. However, because there were three other candidates on the ballot, he received only 40 percent of the popular vote, a situation that many Southerners considered untenable and which led South Carolina to secede from the Union on December 20. Six other slave-holding states—Mississippi, Florida, Alabama, Georgia, Louisiana, and Texas—followed suit within a few weeks.

Convinced that the new president would ruin the South economically, possibly by freeing the slaves, the seven seceded states sent representatives to Montgomery, Alabama, a month prior to Lincoln's March 4, 1861, inauguration to form a new nation and draft a new constitution. They elected Jefferson Davis, a senator from Mississippi and secretary of war during Franklin Pierce's administration, as president of the Confederate States of America.

The disposition of federal property, especially military installations, in the seceded states became an important issue. Of particular interest was a chain of forts protecting the harbor of Charleston, South Carolina. Six days after South Carolina left the Union, the small Federal garrison at Fort Moultrie relocated to Fort Sumter in Charleston Harbor, a move that heightened tensions and resulted in the seizure of nearly all Federal installations in the seceded states.

Despite repeated demands by state officials to surrender the island fortress, garrison commander Maj. Robert Anderson and 127 men continued to occupy Sumter, awaiting reinforcements that were not to come. In the early morning hours of April 12, 1861, secessionists made a final demand that the fort be remanded to state control. Anderson again refused and was told that Sumter would be shelled within the hour. At 4:30 a.m., secessionist artillerists under the command of Brig. Gen. P. G. T. Beauregard fired the first shot of what would be a 34-hour bombardment that ended when the troops occupying Sumter surrendered.

Although Lincoln, in his inaugural address just six weeks earlier, had sought to entice the seceded states to return to the Union, he called for 75,000 volunteers to suppress what many Northerners called "the insurrection." As news of his action spread throughout the South, four other slave states—Virginia, Arkansas, North Carolina, and Tennessee—seceded and joined the Confederacy.

America's greatest tragedy had begun. The stage was set, the boundaries were drawn, and the characters took their places. Kentucky, Missouri, and Maryland voted not to secede. As border states between the warring factions, they became the sites of some of the conflict's early battles as the Union moved to protect its front-line defenses.

To limit the Confederacy's ability to supply its soldiers, Lincoln moved to blockade Southern seaports in 1861 and sent troops to control the South's great river systems. On foot and on horseback, in blue and in gray, the soldiers fought for "honor and glory." At the first battle of Bull Run near Manassas, Virginia, in July 1861, casualties were estimated at 2,900 for Union troops and 2,000 for Confederate soldiers in the one-day engagement. Less than nine months later, in a two-day battle at Shiloh, in southwest Tennessee, the number of killed, wounded, and captured amounted to more than 13,000 for the North and 10,700 for the South.

Casualties continued to escalate on both sides. Union victories in July 1863 at Gettysburg, Pennsylvania, and Vicksburg, Mississippi, marked the military turning points of the war. From then until the conflict's end in April 1865, the South—strangled by blockades and reeling from inflation and internal political strife—was unable to overcome the Union's tremendous advantage in industrial might and manpower.

In dedicating the national soldiers' cemetery at Gettysburg in November 1863, a few months after the battle in which combined casualties exceeded 51,000, Abraham Lincoln answered the question that Americans on both sides of the conflict had long been asking as they struggled to understand the reasons for the appalling bloodshed. "They gave their lives," Lincoln said, "that this nation might live."

Susan Robb's Confederate Appliqué Quilt

According to her descendants, Susan Robb made this quilt in honor of her two stepsons, William Henry and Theodore, who volunteered to serve in the Confederate army. At the time, Susan and her husband, Henry, were living in Phillips County, Arkansas, and had two younger sons at home, Aaron B. and Thomas J. In Susan's elaborate appliqué and embroidered quilt, she depicted a Confederate view of the War Between the States that was probably related by her stepsons. The ranks of soldiers, rifles on their shoulders, are shown marching in step behind flag bearers under the Confederate banners.

Both flags are Confederate. The flag with the circle of stars is a variant of the Confederacy's first National Flag, which was unveiled on March 4, 1861. The flag was modeled after one of the earliest flags of the United States. Southerners likened their struggle against the North to the American colonists fighting the British in the American War for Independence. As additional states joined the Confederacy in 1861, new stars were added. Susan Robb's banner was the most common variant—a circle of stars surrounding a larger star in the center.

However, because the first National Flag was often confused in battle with the Union's Stars and Stripes, the Confederacy adopted a new banner known as the Battle Flag in October 1861. It is the better known Confederate flag and featured a blue St. Andrew's cross, edged in white and bearing thirteen white stars, that was set on a red field. With many flag makers working in isolation in remote towns, there were almost as many variations of both flags as there were flag makers and Confederate regiments. Susan Robb's Battle Flag does not conform to the official design, but she may have taken artistic license based on the color and amount of cloth she had on hand.

Howard Madaus, an authority on Civil War flags and symbols, made the following

observations after examining a photograph of Susan Robb's quilt:

"Both units depicted are Confederate, based on the flags, although the flag at the head of the column of troops uniformed in gray jackets and sky-blue trousers is a variant design of the Confederate Battle Flag. In regard to the uniforms and the cannons depicted in the quilt, nothing is distinctive that would relate them to any region or a specific unit."

Madaus found the eagle and stork locked in combat to be an interesting motif, one that was evidently inspired by an emblem on Continental currency. "The Continental three-dollar bill issued in late 1775 and early 1776 carried two birds in combat, with the eagle as the aggressor. The motto on the bill was 'Exitus in Dubio Est' (The outcome is in doubt"). As the secession movement or 'War for Southern Independence' was sometimes compared to the 1776-1783 struggle for independence from Britain, it is easy to see why the symbol would be borrowed for reuse, though I have not seen it repeated in any other Confederate or Southern 'document,' nor am I aware of its use on any of the various issues of Confederate or Southern state currencies."

If Susan Robb made this quilt at the midpoint of the conflict, when its outcome was still in doubt, perhaps

FACING PAGE AND DETAILS ABOVE
Susan Robb, maker
Possibly Arkansas, Texas, or Mississippi
c. 1863-1865
Cotton; appliqué, reverse appliqué, and embroidery
77˝ x 81˝
Collection of The Museum of Texas Tech University, Lubbock

Continental three-dollar bill, 1775-1776.

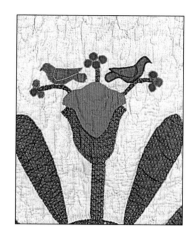

Details of Susan Robb's Confederate Appliqué Quilt.

her positioning of the stork represented the South in the power position over the Union eagle and was her own hopeful wish for a Southern victory. Her stepson William Henry Robb served with the Arkansas Mounted Rifles Company A, but Theodore Robb's military records have not been located. The family said he saw action in Tennessee.

More than 100 years later, the quilt was donated to The Museum of Texas Tech University, where Betty Mills was curator at the time. "When I first saw it," she said, "I described it as an example of 'dedicated stitchery.' I marveled at the maker's ability to stitch with thread and cloth, the facial features, uniform details, and equipment. The birds, cherries, and stars that fill the appliqué blocks were as fascinating to study as the central pictorial panel. According to the family, the quilt was stolen for a time, and the family advertised, appealing for its safe return. And one night, the quilt was found tossed over a bush in a pasture near the owner's home. Soon after, the quilt was donated to the museum."

The Susan Robb quilt has appeared in a number of quilt publications since the 1970s, but the central scene was incorrectly interpreted as depicting regiments of Union and Confederate soldiers. By verifying the Confederate origin of the two flags, we can assume the regiments Susan Robb chose to include were both Confederate, but the drama unfolding in the appliqué scene remains a mystery worth pursuing.

STAYING IN STYLE

QUILTS THAT HAVE become keepsakes are remnants of history and provide insight into the lives of our ancestors. By studying these relics of the past, we can obtain glimpses of our ancestors' homes, their tastes, and their abilities. As we look at the designs and other characteristics of the quilts, we can begin to link them to the people who made them. It is a way of discovering our heritage.

The quiltmaker who lived in the middle of the nineteenth century chose a quilt design with care, knowing that it would require many hours of hand sewing and she wanted a quilt to make her proud. It was a demanding task to furnish bedding for a family, but the duty was accompanied by a certain amount of pleasure and entertainment. While the best quilts were made with care, those for everyday use were not expected to be masterpieces of workmanship or design, nor were they made of the finest material. Nevertheless, their patterns could be sprightly and the colorful fabrics skillfully arranged. Even utility quilts became works of beauty when thoughtful choices of patterns and fabrics were made.

Time and cost were not the only considerations when undertaking a quilt. Just as clothing fashions changed from year to year and interior furnishings gradually evolved from decade to decade, so it was with quilts. First one type of bedcover and then another became the fashion of the time, and quiltmakers accepted the fickle dictates of style. Americans still looked to Europe for the latest modes of dress and decorating, but they tempered them with New World ingenuity and adaptation. The colonists had brought quilt patterns from England that were suitable for silk fabric and sewn together in the template method of piecing (turning and basting the cloth edges over a paper pattern and whipping the creased edges together). That technique was soon replaced by direct

Star Bouquet
Mary M. Leggett, maker
Pennsylvania
1862
95″ x 77 1/2″
Edith A. Sturzenegger, owner

seaming of the pieces, which came about through New England practicality.

The main bedchambers in the more affluent households were fitted with linens appropriate to the family's circumstances. The quilts reflected changing fashion tastes and styles from one decade to another. They ranged from wholecloth glazed wool, copperplate print, and whitework with stuffing to silk (template-pieced), crewel or silk embroidered, chintz appliqué, album, appliqué, and pieced quilts. Many of the quilts were luxury articles that were either purchased or made within the household at considerable time and expense, sometimes with the assistance of slave or itinerant seamstresses.

The whitework quilt was a quilt of exceptional beauty. The top was made of several panels that were seamed together, then quilted in various motifs with close quilting in the background. Frequently, extra cotton was stuffed into certain areas from the underside of the quilt to heighten the sculptured effect. Fine quilting and stuffing could turn plain white material into an elegant work of art.

Chintz, a cotton fabric with a glazed finish, gained great popularity in the period before the war. At first it was used in medallion-type quilts with an appliquéd center design surrounded by borders in a style similar to the work of English quiltmakers. The medallion format was eventually replaced by smaller blocks appliquéd with chintz cutouts of flowers, birds, and leaves. This method was especially practical when more than one person was involved in

Detail of Star Bouquet Quilt, an example of a silk template-pieced quilt.

making the quilt. When the collecting of all manner of objects was in vogue, it was natural for quiltmakers to collect blocks from their friends and relatives. Signatures, dates, and inscriptions were sometimes added to the friendship and album blocks in the same manner in which they were collected for autograph albums.

When appliqué became the style of choice, quiltmakers had access to an abundance of cloth that was manufactured in the United States. Red and green small-patterned prints and solids, with smaller amounts of pink and yellow, were favored for making stunning floral appliqué quilts. Pieced-block patterns began to increase in number as styles evolved from the large four-unit compositions to smaller block arrangements.

Even in the more modest homes at least one quilt was kept apart to use when company came. It may have been the quilt made by a bride prior to her marriage—when she put her best skills and dreams into its making—or perhaps it was a fine quilt made by an ancestor and highly prized.

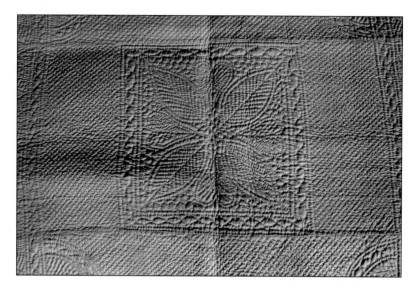

Wholecloth Wool Quilt
Maker unknown
Probably northeastern
United States
c. 1800-1830
77" x 72"
Collection of Memphis
Pink Palace Museum,
Memphis, Tennessee

Improved methods of agriculture and the introduction of exotic plants fostered widespread interest in gardening and horticulture. As settlers moved inland, they made concerted efforts to civilize and beautify their new surroundings. Emily Murrell, a young girl from Tennessee, wrote in her diary while visiting an uncle in Oklahoma in 1850: "I quilted a little while, we then mounted our ponys & rode by the mill from thence round thro' woods & prairies to gather flowers. . . . I found two new ones. . . . I pressed one of each variety, which I shall put in my 'Herbarium.'" It was natural for this botanical interest to be applied to quiltmaking.

By the middle of the nineteenth century, appliqué work was often the style chosen for the "best" quilt, sometimes combined with pieced work. The rose was a favorite motif used in dozens of variations and combinations of flowers, buds, leaves, and vines. Rose of Sharon, the name applied to many quilt designs, had its origin in a Bible passage that was a favorite of young women because of its romantic connotations:

I am a rose of Sharon, a lily of the valleys.
As a lily among brambles, so is my love among maidens.

The rose was often chosen for a wedding quilt, and that quilt would be carefully cared for through the years. In addition to the rose, many other designs were taken from

Rose Tree, appliquéd
Maker unknown
c. 1850
East Tennessee
Collection of Olde
Deery Inn,
Blountville,
Tennessee

nature, including Cockscomb and Currant, Tulip, Oak Leaf and Acorn, Oak Leaf and Cherries, Rose Tree, and Tree of Life, to name a few.

Another type of appliqué was derived from a European folded-paper cutting technique that resulted in a "snowflake" design. When cut from red cloth and applied to a white background, the design made a striking presentation. Sometimes an itinerant peddler of household wares cut a pattern for the mistress of the house in exchange for a night's lodging.

Few quilt patterns were available through publications, and it wasn't until the late nineteenth century that many quilt designs were given names. Prior to the War, *Godey's Lady's Book* and other periodicals occasionally presented articles on quiltmaking derived

Cherry Mansion Star Quilt, pieced.

from British sources that contained designs suitable primarily for silk. For the most part, quilt patterns came from family and friends and were shared in letters that crossed oceans, mountains, and plains. A clever miss carefully studied a new design and then drew it from memory when she had the opportunity.

Mothers and family members had a duty to train young girls in the necessary needlework skills that would be required of them throughout their lives. After practicing the simplest steps in making patchwork, the novices gradually improved their ability as they undertook progressively more complicated projects. By the time they reached adolescence, the girls were expected to have completed several quilts for their hope chests. Variable Star, Young Man's Fancy, Turkey Tracks, Pine Tree, Reel, North Carolina Lily, Melon Patch, and Spinning Ball were some of the popular patterns of the mid-nineteenth century.

Simpler patterns were favored for everyday quilts and for use by beginners. Four

Patch, Nine Patch, Irish Chain, Basket, and Windmill are found in endless variations. The scraps from household sewing and even the less worn parts of discarded garments provided variety in color and contrast when combined with a few pieces of store-bought cloth. The familiar shapes were easily stitched together whenever a few minutes could be spared from more strenuous chores. The quiltmaker valued those respites when she could quietly gather her thoughts to herself.

Since winters in the South were relatively mild, houses were not well heated; hence, the larger the family, the more bedding was needed. Quilt production was an ongoing process, and the prudent housewife prolonged the use of her linens to the fullest extent possible. When a quilt was worn beyond practical use, it could be recovered with a new top and back to give it added life. A worn blanket or coverlet made an acceptable filler for the inside of a quilt, and even old clothing and other unorthodox materials were often put into quilts.

Quilting frames were common to almost every home, whether a large plantation

Quilt frame from the collection of Olde Deery Inn, Blountville, Tennessee.

These implements, known as cards, were used for combing cotton to make quilt batting.

house or small cabin. The frames came in almost endless styles, from well-crafted fine furniture on upright legs to single rails hung from the ceiling by rope and pulley. Family members, hired help, and slaves found their places around the quilting frames on a regular schedule. Occasionally a bee and husking frolic provided entertainment for a large gathering and offered work in a pleasurable setting, good food, games, and even opportunities for courting. For these affairs, the hostess would put out her best quilts and share any new patterns she may have received.

But soon after the first shots fired at Fort Sumter plunged the nation into war, life in the South changed forever.

The quilts that survived the Civil War period do not present an accurate sampling of the bedding of the time since they tend to be the "best" quilts, those especially prized by their owners. The ordinary quilts were used daily, and when they were worn beyond practicality, they were discarded or used to cover farm equipment or bedsprings. Nevertheless, those quilts that remain provide a window to the past.

Back of whitework quilt showing coarsely woven quilt lining and holes where extra cotton was stuffed into quilted areas.
Collection of Z. C. and Sarah Key Patten.

These surviving relics made by the hands of Southern quiltmakers are representative of the broad array of styles that were popular during the antebellum period. The medallion, silk template-pieced, silk embroidered, and whitework wholecloth quilts display the influence of European stylemakers. Appliqué and chintz work, while following fashions from abroad, soon acquired distinctive regional characteristics, but it was in the development of the pieced patterns that American quiltmakers made their greatest contributions.

THE FABRIC OF THEIR LIVES

DOMESTIC LIFE in the South changed dramatically when the Civil War broke out. Seaports, once important conduits for imported British and French printed cottons and silks, were blockaded by the Union. Peddlers who formerly plied their wares along Southern byways did not venture out of Northern cities. Local cotton gins and textile mills, where Southern women sent their wool and cotton to be manufactured into thread, became military targets.

As Southern men began enlisting for military service by the tens of thousands, clothing the troops became as important as arming them. In the North, the United States Sanitary Commission organized massive sewing campaigns and fairs to meet the needs of Union soldiers. In the South, the women were just as determined but their efforts were more localized.

On October 4, 1861, Margaret Stakely, who was living in Searcy, Arkansas, wrote to her sister in Tennessee: "When I hear that there is work to do, I put on my bonnet, get my thimble, and away to the church, which is the place the ladies generally meet. We can either sew there, or carry the work home with us. I have helped make tents, pants, blankets, etc. etc. We have been making blankets of carpeting and lining them with cotton goods, and it is feared that when the carpets are all cut up, there will not be enough to supply all the soldiers."

On January 6, 1862, Carrie Stakely, who was living in Madisonville, Tennessee, wrote to her sister Martha about a flag she had made: "Came home then and sat up late, cutting letters for a motto to be sewed on a flag for Pryor's company. Thursday morning I went out to see Letitia Humphries who is sick with Typhoid Fever and rheumatism, and that night Ada and I sat up until 3 o'clock to finish the flag. Several of the girls pronounced it the handsomest one sent from this place. It was made of Oil Calico, Blue Gingham and jaconet, the only material we could get. Had 13 stars in a circle in the blue, and in the white stripe the sentiment "Liberty or Death" put on, with the words "Liberty" and "Death" both arched, and the "Or" between them. The shape of the letters was very pretty I think. Mr. Barkley suggested the motto."

On April 22, 1862, the *Knoxville Daily Register* carried the following appeal for clothing needed by soldiers: "Gray cassimere pants, shirts, homemade shoes, long boots for cavalry, heavy grained boots for infantry, brown flannel overshirts, linsey overshirts." Women shouldered much of the burden for supplying clothing and bedding.

Carrie Stakely received a letter dated April 4, 1862, from Mr. J. I. Wright, acknowledging the donation of bedding to his company: "I received your note, accompanying comforts & blankets sent to my men only on yesterday. The clothes

Linsey Dress
Unknown quiltmaker from Blair family
Roane County, Tennessee
1860s
Checked linsey dress lined with printed cotton cloth
Mary Browning, owner

Detail of striped linsey skirt made in East Tennessee during the 1860s.

reached us the day they were started. My men did stand much in need of these articles at the time sent, and they were received by us with the same gratitude as if there had been fifty times as many. We will gratefully remember our kind benefactress when far away from the sweet endearments of Home. My company is now pretty well supplied with necessary clothing . . . . Pray for the spiritual and temporal welfare of the soldier & his safe return under peaceful sky to the quiet of Home."

The massive sewing campaign coincided with shortages of the very goods the women needed to produce the supplies. The situation demanded resourcefulness, diligence, and pride. Lucy Virginia French wrote: "I am ready and willing to cut up all my carpets to make 'covers' or blankets for them if necessary. . . . When I spoke of taking up my parlor carpet one of them said. 'Well I'll be doggone if that ain't too fine a carpet to cut up for soldiers,' but I had it taken up nevertheless."

Women who a few years earlier might have whiled away an afternoon in their parlors, sewing some fancy work or pondering which dressmaker to hire, now found

Linsey skirt. The rough, scratchy cloth was uncomfortable to wear.

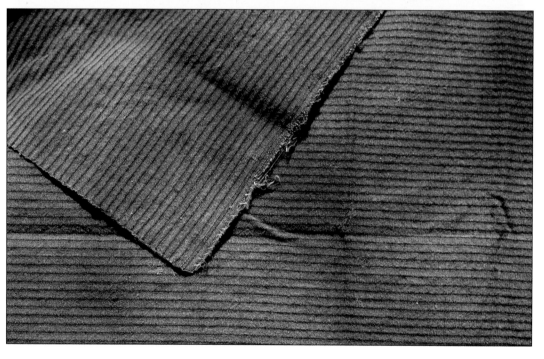

Remnant of linsey, cotton warp and wool weft. In Tennessee and other interior regions during the Civil War, linsey cloth was woven on home looms.

themselves patching dresses to extend their usefulness or making their own linsey dresses, and being quite proud of it. Home-manufactured cloth known as linsey was a rough, cheap cloth made of a cotton warp and a wool weft. In the years before the war, many slaves wore this humble cloth. When Harriet Brent Jacobs reported on her life as a slave girl in 1861, she recalled, "the linsey-woolsey dress given me every winter by Mrs. Flint. How I hated it. It was one of the badges of slavery."

Robert Shepherd, at age ninety-one, was interviewed for the WPA Federal Writers' Project. The former slave from Athens, Georgia, remembered the making of cloth on the farm, "De cloth for 'most all of de clothes was made at home. Master Joe raised lots of sheep and de wool was used to make cloth for de winter clothes. Us had a great long loom house where some of de slaves didn't do nothin' but weave cloth. Some carded bats, some done de spinnin', and dere was more of 'em to do de sewin'.

Negro women who remained with their Southern masters taught the white women of the house to spin, card, and weave. Dolly Lunt Burge wrote about her day's activities in her diary on November 12, 1864: "Warped and put in dresses for the loom [dressed the loom]. Oh, this blockade gives us work to do for all hands."

A Georgia woman described her friend's "Confederate" dress thusly: "She has a black linsey dress that she dyed herself and it is a beautiful black. She seems to have succeeded remarkably well with her experiments."

Fannie Stakely, living in Magnolia, Alabama, wrote her sister in East Tennessee: "If you get homespun, let it be almost anything before blue [the color of Northern uniforms]; our neighbors would almost drum us out of service. They make their dresses purple and white or brown and purple. Mother has a dress of Georgia stripes that is brown and white." Resourcefulness was both patriotic and required.

Prior to the war, most towns in the interior of the South had a cotton gin and many had large textile mills. The cotton gin, patented in 1794, had essentially eliminated the home spinning of thread, especially cotton thread. As women sent their corn to the mill to be ground, so did they send their cotton to the spinning mill to be

carded and made into thread. These textile factories were essential to the
Confederate cause and became easy targets for Union offensives; thus, spinning
wheels and combing cards were brought out of storage in attics and barns
throughout the South.

On November 26, 1862, Amanda McDowell wrote woefully: "We thought it
odd when we had to spin wool, but it will be something extra indeed when we have
to spin cotton. There seems to be no prospect of peace."

Harriet Strother of Barnesville, Georgia, a town near Macon, wrote Sam
Caldwell on January 29, 1862: "I am sorry I did not know you needed cards. I could
have got them in the summer at $1.00 but they are all gone now. I have one pr
only. I card a large pile (half bushel) of rolls every night to help along the next
days work."

*Detail of pieced linsey
quilt, probably made in
Middle Tennessee,
c. 1880, of wool, cotton,
and linsey fabrics.*

The textile mills and carding factories that managed to stay open charged exorbitant prices for precious yarn and thread. One Georgia woman wrote: "I wish we could spin by magic. It would assist us very much if we were near a carding factory. I am told there are plenty around this place, but I do not know what they charge per pound. What do you think of yarn selling for thirty to thirty-five a bunch in Marietta?"

In areas occupied by Northern troops, women had to swear allegiance to the Union in order to purchase the goods they needed, even when they knew the storekeeper was administering the oath under duress. The oath of allegiance stated: "I, _____, do solemnly swear, in the presence of Almighty God, that I will henceforth faithfully support and defend the Constitution of the United States, and the Union of States thereunder; and that I will, in like manner, abide by and faithfully support all Laws and Proclamations which have been made during the existing rebellion, with reference to the emancipation of slaves, so help me God."

Taking the oath meant keeping a house, a job, or not being banished. It also meant maintaining a family's meager supply of food and cloth. For women who had witnessed the atrocities of war firsthand or whose loved ones had fallen in battle, this oath was dreadful. Mary Jane Reynolds could not bring herself to say the oath, so she devised a way to circumvent the requirement, which she described in a letter to her husband Simeon D. Reynolds in March 1864: "We are pretty quiet now. Mrs. Franklin is here, came last night. Had been to Loudon to pick out some calico for Mr. Kline to buy [for her]. That is the way the ladies get out of taking the oath, but Andersons sell to almost anyone."

And then on April 1, 1864, Mrs. Reynolds wrote: "They say they are not near so particular about selling goods as they were at first there. They [used to ask] a person if they were loyal, now they ask them if they will trade."

The heartache and pain of the war lingered long after the men returned home or were buried, long after the Union soldiers headed north, and long after the Confederate prisoners were released. Sadness tempered with pride remained, but gruesome memories

never faded. In 1910, Mary
High Prince, a former spy
for the Confederacy, made a
pillow cover from fabric
scraps of textiles her friends
had made during the war,
and on the pillow she
stitched these lines:

Hoorah! for the home spun
dresses we southern ladies
wore in time of the war.
Ev'ry piece here.
Sad memories it brings
back to me.
For our hearts was weary
and restless.
And our life was full of care.
The burden laid up on us
seemed greater than
we could bear.

Mary Prince
1910
Age 70 yrs.

Commemorative Pillow
Mary High Prince, maker
Raus, Bedford County, Tennessee
1910
Homespun cotton fabrics; pieced
work and embroidery
19˝ x 19˝
Emeline P. Gist, owner

QUILTS
GONE TO WAR

Mellichamp Quilt

At the age of thirty-two, George Holyoke left his wife and farm to enlist in the United States Army on September 1, 1862, in Rock Island, Illinois. He joined Company K of the Forty-fifth Regiment of Illinois Volunteer Infantry, which participated extensively in General Grant's campaign against Vicksburg, Mississippi. Later in the war, Company K served in the Atlanta campaign and with General Sherman on his March to the Sea. From Savannah, Georgia, the Forty-fifth campaigned northward through the Carolinas and, after the surrender of the armies of Generals Lee and Johnston in April 1865, marched to Washington, D.C., to participate in the Grand Review of the Army. George Holyoke was honorably discharged in Washington on June 3, 1865. Assuming that he did not spend much time away from the regiment during his three years of service, he witnessed many of the war's major battles and was fortunate to return home safely.

At some point during the war, George Holyoke sent his wife a prized trophy: a quilt that he had spotted in an army camp in Louisiana or Mississippi. Holyoke said he had bought it from a Union soldier who was using it for bedding. Mrs. Holyoke, one would imagine, unfolded the quilt and gasped in disbelief. She had not seen that style of quilt before, but she recognized the glazed

Mellichamp family and others, makers
Probably James Island, South Carolina
1850-1855
Cotton fabric; cut-out-chintz appliqué
72″ x 93″
Collection of Kansas State Historical Society, Topeka; gift of Mrs. George Holyoke

chintz from which the appliqué designs had
been cut as being fine imported cloth.
Thirty-five squares and nineteen
triangles were joined by a thin chintz
border print, and fifty-four names were
inscribed in ink on the quilt.

As Mrs. Holyoke peered at those names, all
written by the same hand, she must have wondered
who they were. The Mellichamps—men and women—
were the largest group represented, totaling fourteen names in
all. The Rivers family had seven names inscribed, and the
Cromwells and Hinsons each had four. Who was the intended recipient of the beautiful
quilt? Who was grieving over its loss?

After the war, George T. Holyoke was ordained as a Congregational minister and
served at churches in Galesburg, Illinois, and Axtell and Topeka, Kansas. He died in
1895. Mrs. Holyoke, who lived to the age of ninety-four, preserved the quilt well and, in
1924, gave it to the Kansas Historical Society for safekeeping as a relic of the Civil War.
At her request, the curators tried to locate the quilt's original Southern owner by
investigating the list of inscribed names, but they were unsuccessful.

The quilt, still in very good condition, has often been shown in Kansas Historical
Society exhibits and catalogs. Recently, William S. Scott, a Civil War enthusiast with a
particular interest in the Forty-fifth Illinois Volunteers, was asked to research George
Holyoke's military records as well as those of the men whose names appear on the quilt.
He determined that the quilt was probably made in the small village of St. Andrews, on
James Island, South Carolina. Twenty of the names on the quilt appeared on the 1860

United States census of St. Andrews, and others were listed in nearby Charleston. The ages of those persons in 1860 ranged from fifteen to sixty-eight, which means the quilt dated from no earlier than 1845.

Researching the male names on the quilt, Scott found that the war had been hard on the Mellichamp family. Only Stiles Rivers Mellichamp and Robert E. Mellichamp survived the war. A "W. A." Mellichamp was given a medical disability discharge in October 1862, while W. S. Mellichamp died as the result of a wound and E. A. and James M. Mellichamp both died of illness in Northern prisons. No Mellichamps served with any South Carolinian units that were involved in the Vicksburg campaign.

If George Holyoke obtained the quilt in Louisiana or Mississippi, how did the quilt get there? Only Stiles Mellichamp had ventured far afield, surveying in northern Alabama and Georgia. That would roughly have placed him in the path of the Forty-fifth Illinois, but not until the spring of 1864. Could Mrs. Holyoke have been mistaken about where her husband obtained the quilt? Perhaps it was given as a gift by Eliza O. Mellichamp (age eighteen in 1860) to a sweetheart that served in Mississippi. Or perhaps it belonged to one of the less fortunate members of the community and was lost during the Carolina campaign of 1865 and came to Kansas as a souvenir of war.

To mark the Union victory, the War Department ordered a Grand Review of the Armies in Washington, D.C., in May 1865.

The Cherry Mansion Star Quilt

Cherry Mansion, an impressive house high on the banks of the Tennessee River near Savannah, in West Tennessee, was built in the mid-nineteenth century by David Robinson. The homestead was noted for its landscaping, with five grass terraces leading down to the river and beautiful gardens of roses and boxwoods. It was the setting for elegant parties and reflected the comfortable lifestyle of an affluent Southern family. But all of that changed when Civil War conflicts shattered lives and land in the vicinity of Shiloh.

Gen. Ulysses S. Grant selected the Robinson estate for his headquarters during the six months he conducted the Shiloh campaign for the Union forces. Home owners had no choice but to acquiesce when their property was requisitioned for use by military personnel, and they never knew in what condition they would find it when they returned.

During the period of General Grant's occupancy a colorful star quilt covered the bed in which he slept. The nine blocks of pieced stars in red, yellow, and green combine with the

Union Gen. Ulysses S. Grant

FACING PAGE
Maker unknown
c. 1850-1860
Cotton fabric; pieced work
109″ x 100″
Collection of the Tennessee State Museum, Nashville; gift of Mrs. W. J. Hagin III, given in memory of Louise Stacy Keller

white background to make a striking quilt enhanced with appropriate quilting motifs. The general is said to have admired it greatly.

The quilt was passed down in the Robinson family, eventually coming to Mrs. W. J. Hagin Jr. from a descendant.

In her autobiography, *Recollections of 92 Years: 1824-1916*, Elizabeth Avery Meriweather described an interview with General Grant during the occupation of Memphis after the battle of Shiloh. The General had issued a decree banishing any person who was found corresponding with the enemy. Mrs. Meriweather's husband was a major in the Confederate Army, and a disgruntled local Northern sympathizer, a Mrs. Hickey, was attempting to see that Mrs. Meriweather was evicted from her estate. In an effort to keep her home, Mrs. Meriweather requested an interview with General Grant and, while waiting to see him, wondered if he would even listen to the wife of a Confederate officer.

"Of course he will listen to her," replied the soldier [in attendance]. "General Grant is a gentleman and he knows a lady when he sees one. Several of us saw Mrs. Hickey drive this lady off [from her home] with a carving fork."

The general did, indeed, write an order to the provost marshal protecting Mrs. Meriweather and allowing her to retain her home. The order was canceled, however, when General Sherman came to Memphis. Sherman, in retaliation for Confederates firing on Union gunboats on the Mississippi River, banished ten wives of rebel soldiers, among them Mrs. Meriweather.

Though General Grant waged total war on the battlefield, when he occupied Cherry Mansion, he behaved almost as if he were a visitor, showing respect for the rights and property of others, even those of the enemy.

Barbara Broyles's Quilt

Mathias and Barbara Lotspeich Broyles decided in the 1840s to leave their home in Rhea County, Tennessee, for the challenge of a new business venture. They packed up their household goods, including fine stuffed-work quilts for which Rhea County has become famous, and moved to the Cumberland Plateau near Crossville. There they operated a stagecoach stop and tavern (inn) on the route from Knoxville to Nashville.

Barbara Lotspeich Broyles, maker
Rhea County, Tennessee
c. 1840
White cotton fabric; quilted and stuffed
81″ x 77″
Bettye Broyles, owner

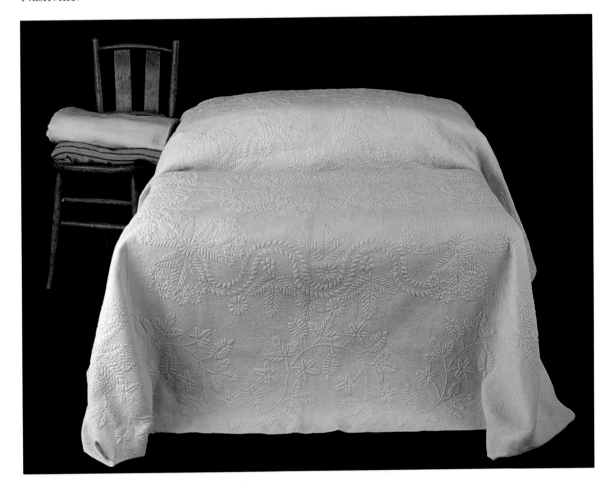

Armies on the move during the Civil War had difficulty procuring supplies at each encampment. For that reason, it was necessary for individual soldiers to carry whatever equipment and personal belongings were needed for their survival and comfort. In the event of a rapid advance or retreat, bedding and clothing were the first items to be discarded. Throughout the countryside where military activity was occurring, the need to obtain food was followed closely by the need to requisition bedding.

Barbara Broyles, in her compassion for the Rebel cause, loaned some of her homemade quilts to Confederate soldiers camped nearby in 1862. In most instances, the items loaned were never seen again, but such was not the case for Barbara's quilts. "The soldiers were unkind enough to return her quilts," her grandson reported later. Unkind? Yes, a soldier who used one of the quilts was infected with typhus and the bacteria was passed on to the Broyleses when the quilts were returned. Barbara and her husband died from the disease within four days of each other. Surprisingly, however, the quilt was not destroyed because of its deadly past and became a survivor of the Civil War.

FACING PAGE AND RIGHT
Details of Barbara Broyles's Quilt.

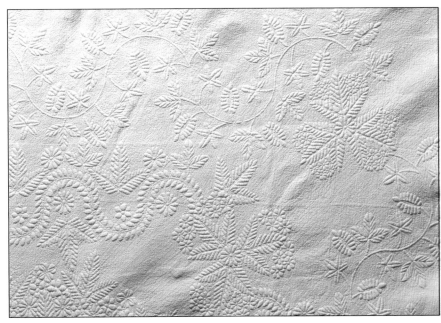

The Poncho Quilt — Rose Tree

A Confederate soldier returning home in 1864 sold this quilt to John R. Nelson of Knoxville, Tennessee. Until his death in 1923, Nelson enjoyed recounting the tale of a quilt that became a soldier's salvation.

According to the story, a Southern soldier traveling on foot snatched the quilt from a clothesline outside a Virginia farmhouse. By the time he reached Knoxville days later, he was cold, exhausted, and penniless. The city's police officers at that time were rounding up homeless soldiers and bringing them before local judges, who charged them with vagrancy and sent them to jail. Constable John R. Nelson, a Confederate sympathizer, took pity on the young soldier and offered to buy the quilt. Once the transaction was completed, the soldier, with some spare change in his pocket, was no longer a vagrant and was able to go on his way. Nelson's descendants have often wondered just how much he paid for the quilt. Some think it might have been as little as fifty cents.

The image of a soldier slogging through the crowded streets of Knoxville, his gaunt, muddied face protruding from a slit cut in the white quilt with red and green appliquéd flowers, is quite sad and probably true. Verifying the details of such accounts that have been handed down through the years is difficult, but there are

Although Union sentiment ran high in East Tennessee, the city of Knoxville, seen from Keith's Hills in this 1863 engraving, remained in Confederate hands until September 1863, when it was occupied by Northern troops led by Gen. Ambrose Burnside.

FACING PAGE
Maker unknown
Possibly Tennessee
Cotton fabric; appliqué
92″ x 72″
Ella Ree Bounds, owner

clues in this quilt that support the story. Someone carefully repaired the slit, using solid-colored fabrics that closely match the original yellow and red. The background white fabric was inserted into the opening and sewn down. The original slash had destroyed two appliqué blooms in the center, but the seamstress repairing the quilt had to look no farther than the outer corners of the quilt to find flowers identical to the demolished appliqué blooms.

The seamstress's solution is not immediately obvious until one examines the quilt closely and finds that a bloom is missing from two corner Rose Tree blocks. The seamstress simply removed the appliqué blooms and attached them in the repaired center area where the slit had been made.

LEFT AND FACING PAGE
Details of The Poncho Quilt—Rose Tree.
The vertical slit shown on the facing page was repaired using a rose bloom from the quilt block at left.

Medallion Quilt

The destruction of human life, animals, and the land during the war was hideous and unrelenting. Corpses lay among the wounded, with Confederates and Yankees sometimes mixed indifferently together. The moans and screams, the mud and dust, the flies, and the stench created a hellish tableau, yet merciful healers often could be seen administering to the injured, the sick, and the dying.

In her journal, Mary Chesnut described conditions in improvised hospitals in Virginia and South Carolina, the unstinting efforts of the nurses and volunteers, the endless difficulty in obtaining supplies, the heartache, and the sadness. Women unable to provide hospital service energetically raised money and sought medical supplies, sewed, knit, rolled

DETAIL ABOVE AND FACING PAGE
Maker unknown
Probably Mecklenburg County, North Carolina
c. 1830-1840
Cotton fabric, glazed chintz; appliqué
85″ x 82″
Virginia Williams Kennickell, owner

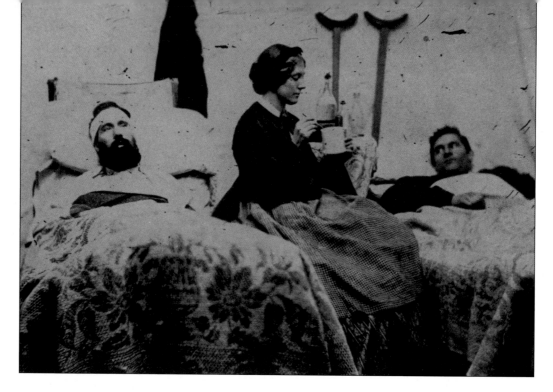

Sickness and disease exacted a fearful toll among soldiers on both sides of the conflict. Many women throughout the North and the South served as nurses and volunteers in hospitals and elsewhere, assisting physicians with medical procedures, providing patient care, procuring supplies, washing clothes, cooking for the troops, and performing many other tasks. Above, a nurse tends to wounded patients in a military hospital in Nashville, Tennessee, during the Union occupation of the city.

bandages, and did whatever they could, knowing that any casualty could well be one of their loved ones.

Physicians who volunteered their services to the Confederate Army knew they would be working under difficult conditions in inadequate facilities, with meager equipment, limited supplies, and unskilled assistants. Nonetheless, they valiantly attempted to heal the wounded and comfort the dying. Sickness and disease proved to be even more deadly than guns, and countless soldiers on both sides lost their lives as the result of poor sanitation and inadequate nutrition.

Dr. Robert Wilkerson of Buncombe County, North Carolina, knew that medical services would be badly needed wherever fighting occurred and felt it was his obligation to be there. Having previously received his training at the Medical College of

Philadelphia, Dr. Wilkerson was made a lieutenant in Company K of the Sixtieth North Carolina Regiment. While searching the battlefield for survivors after a certain bloody engagement, he came upon a dead mule that still bore a saddle and a quilt that served as a saddle blanket. Dr. Wilkerson recognized the quilt as being of a type that could be found in a fine Southern home and salvaged it from the mule. Later, the quilt was mended and laundered by his mother, Elizabeth Maxwell Cooper. Within the family it came to be known as the War Quilt, and it was always reserved for special company.

Nothing is known of the quilt's origin, but it is in the style of chintz quilts made in the 1830s and has fabric identical to three quilts made in the vicinity of Mecklenburg County, North Carolina at that time. The oval center of chintz flowers set on a white background is offset by four small outer triangles of flowers and surrounded by two chintz and two white borders, all of which are finely quilted.

Dr. Wilkerson knew a good quilt when he saw one, even if it was on a dead mule!

Polly's Rose Quilt

There was excitement at the Timberlake farm near Parker's Crossroads, Tennessee, on December 31, 1862. Louisa Small Timberlake had just given birth to her first child, a son. Phoeba Small and her daughter, Mary, had come to assist with the birth and, of course, admire the baby. During breakfast the next morning, as the family became aware of activity outside, Confederate Gen. Nathan Bedford Forrest rode up to the window to announce that the family would have to leave immediately. His soldiers were pulling up the fence paling around the house, and lines already had been drawn for the battle of Parker's Crossroads, as it came to be known.

It was decided that the family would evacuate to Phoeba's house, which meant crossing enemy lines. While a pass was being issued, the women gathered together a scant few necessities. Mary threw her grandmother's rose quilt across the new mother and child, and four of the family farmhands carried the bed and its occupants to the safe refuge of the Small farm. The baby, appropriately named Battle, survived only a few days.

Louisa Small Timberlake

FACING PAGE
Mary (Polly) Hutchings Small, maker
Pleasant Exchange, Henderson
County, Tennessee
c. 1840
Cotton fabric, some or all home-dyed;
wool thread for embroidery hand-spun
from the quiltmaker's sheep; appliqué
108˝ x 88˝
Kit Jeans Mounger, owner

Edward Timberlake

Willis Timberlake

After the battle, which lasted several hours, the Timberlake house was turned into a field hospital for the wounded. Louisa's quilts and linens were torn up and used for dressings as there was a shortage of medical supplies. The rose quilt was the only one of Louisa's quilts to escape destruction, because it had been taken to Phoeba's farm. As the tide of battle turned against the Southern forces, General Forrest commandeered all of the horses on the Timberlake farm as he beat a rapid retreat back across the Tennessee River.

When word came that Phoeba's son, Willis, was gravely ill in a primitive field hospital in Vicksburg, Mississippi, Mary became determined to bring her brother home. She packed provisions, a feather mattress, and the surviving rose quilt, and hitched up the only remaining mule and a cow to pull the wagon. She was accompanied by Joe Timberlake, a freedman who served as houseman. Vicksburg was 500 miles away, and Mary had no maps to follow and there were no inns at which to rest. Stopping wherever they could, Mary and Joe

Detail of Polly's Rose Quilt.

spent one night with a farm family who had a new baby and were happy to swap a mule for Mary's cow, which somewhat improved the pair's mode of transportation.

At the end of the difficult and dangerous journey, Mary and Joe found Willis still alive and nursed him until he was strong enough to travel. Covering Willis with his grandmother's quilt, they brought him back to Timberlake. Willis eventually recovered and lived a long life, enjoying his children and grandchildren.

The quilt's maker, Polly Hutchings, christened Mary, was five years old in 1779 when she accompanied the party of her grandfather, Col. John Donelson, on the uncharted rivers of Tennessee to reach the Cumberland River at a site that would later become Nashville. When she was twenty-three she married Daniel Small, another member of the Donelson party, and they moved west to Henderson County. It was a hard life on the frontier. Many of their children died in childhood and in 1838 Daniel disappeared on a business trip down the Natchez Trace. Perhaps it was in her grief that Polly made the rose quilt to bring comfort out of her loneliness. Before she died in 1846 she gave the quilt to her daughter-in-law, Phoeba, to be passed on to her namesake, Mary, and future generations.

Edward J. Timberlake's farm, c. 1913. Although the farmhouse no longer stands, descendants of the Timberlake family still live near Parker's Crossroads, in the community of Timberlake, just north of Lexington, Tennessee.

Irish Chain with Appliqué Quilt

Just four years after young John George Bauer (1837-1918) emigrated from Germany and settled in southern Minnesota, the American Civil War broke out. He enlisted in the United States Cavalry on September 10, 1861, and served with a company of mostly German-speaking volunteers attached to the Fifth Iowa Cavalry led by Maj. Carl Schaffer de Boernstein.

Bauer's company patrolled on horseback, guarded bridges, and fought minor battles near Shiloh in April 1862. All in all, the men saw little fierce fighting until May 6, 1862, when Bauer's small group was attacked by the Sixth Confederate Cavalry while patrolling through Weakley County, in northwest Tennessee. The nearest settlement was Lockridge Mill, nothing more than a farm and mill at a crossroads.

John George Bauer

The men were surprised by a superior force of Confederates who were returning from the Nashville area. Seven soldiers of the Fifth Iowa were killed and seventeen were wounded, including John George Bauer, who suffered such a terrible wound that his fellow cavalrymen insisted his arm be amputated. Bauer vehemently rejected the idea and found himself left behind as the rest of his company headed home to Iowa and Minnesota.

Mary Benson Lockridge, who lived in the large white frame house nearby, was a

Confederate sympathizer, but she nursed Bauer's wounds and allowed him to stay with her family until he had recovered sufficiently to return home on his own. When the time came for Bauer to leave, Mary Lockridge draped a quilt over his shoulders to hide the Union blue of his uniform, in the hope that he would be able to slip unnoticed through the Confederate defenses. Indeed, Bauer made contact with Union forces near Paducah, Kentucky, and then traveled to Fort Snelling, Minnesota, where he was discharged from the army on September 16, 1862, having served just one year.

For the rest of his life, John George Bauer retold his tale of the compassionate Christian Southern lady who had come to his aid. Her kindness inspired Bauer to become a Methodist minister, and he was assigned to a circuit of German Methodist churches in the Minnesota River Valley. Bauer died in 1918, leaving the quilt to his daughter, Lydia Bauer, who valued the quilt and its story highly. For a time, she loaned the quilt to the Hennepin County Museum in Minneapolis, but at her death, she willed it to her grandson, John Graber.

In the early 1970s, Graber and his wife, accompanied by their young children, traveled to Tennessee to locate Lockridge Mill. Coincidentally, at the time of the

DETAIL AND FACING PAGE
Mary Benson Lockridge, maker
Lockridge Mill, Weakley County, Tennessee
1850s
Cotton fabric; pieced work; appliqué
84˝ x 72˝
John W. Graber, owner

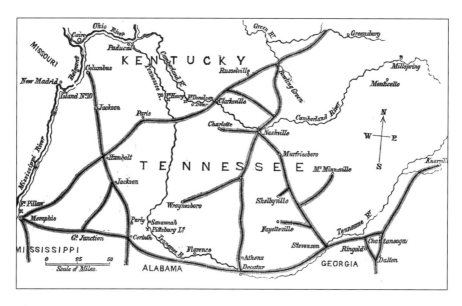

The war in Tennessee and Kentucky.

family's visit, a county historian was compiling data on the battle so that the Tennessee Historical Commission could erect a marker on the site of the one-day engagement. As the historians searched for unmarked graves and a river bridge that figured prominently in the story, John Graber arrived with the quilt and the story of his great-grandfather's fortunate encounter with Mary Lockridge.

In the grand scheme of the Civil War, the battle of Lockridge Mill was no more than a skirmish, yet one young man's life was dramatically affected by the kindness of a woman whose caring for human life outweighed her allegiance to any political cause.

ON THE HOME FRONT

The Cave Hill Farm Quilt — Feathered Star

Nan Kinkead (1837-1925) was a spirited young woman with strong opinions on issues of the day, including support for the secessionist cause. Her problem was that she resided in a pro-Union region of Tennessee, in the foothills of the Appalachian Mountains.

In 1856 Nan's mother, Polly, sent her over the mountains to Asheville, North Carolina, where Nan attended the Holston Conference Female College, a school supported by the Methodist Church. At graduation, her beau, the handsome and debonair Jim Whitney, offered Nan an engagement ring, but she was bothered by Jim's ambivalent feelings about the war. When he chose to enlist as a medical officer with the Union forces, Nan broke off the engagement in disgust and returned to East Tennessee.

At home, the so-called "disturbance" was slow to develop into a full-fledged war. Tennesseans were reluctant to vote to secede, but soon after Abraham Lincoln was inaugurated, he sent a militia to suppress an insurrection at Fort Sumter, South Carolina. That

Mary Ann (Polly) Kinkead

FACING PAGE
Polly Ann Kinkead and her daughters Nan and Rowanna, makers
Hawkins County, Tennessee
1856-1861
Cotton fabric; pieced work
78″ x 62″
Collection of the Carroll Reece Museum, East Tennessee State University, Johnson City; gift of Maryana Smith Huff

proved to be the turning point, and on May 7, 1861, four more slave states, including Tennessee, seceded.

With the young men going off to war or contemplating such action, women Nan's age, of necessity, put off marriage and stayed at home to help their parents maintain the family farm.

In quiet times, Nan and her sister Rowanna, assisted by their mother, Polly, worked on quilts for their dowries. The women often found themselves arguing about the war, whether they wanted to or not. Mr. Kinkead had died years before, leaving Polly to raise their two daughters alone. Polly understood Nan's hatred of the Yankees, but she treasured life and the pursuit of happiness more than anything else. War was evil. War was unkind. No one ended up the winner.

It was on a day when Polly was feeling particularly melancholic that a young, sickly looking man came to her door, asking to be hidden from the Yankees. Since he was not wearing a uniform, Polly was unsure of his motives.

"You're not a deserter, are you?" she asked.

"No, ma'am, I was with some of them prisoners that the Yankee officers were takin' to Knoxville," the man replied. "I slipped away from the guards one night. Been hidin' out, till I can get back to Wythe County."

Polly and Rowanna led the man to the parlor and sat him down in front of their warm fire. Nan was not at home. The two women brought him a tray of food and listened intently to his story. The man needed a place to hide, but a house wouldn't do because bushwhackers were known to walk in, unannounced, to search for deserters hiding inside.

Rowanna immediately thought of the cave in the hill behind the house. Polly urged the visitor to go quickly and handed him a lantern, some matches, and a quilt. "Go through the orchard and up the hill in a straight line from our house to the fence," she told him. "Cross over and the entry to the cave is right there, but almost hidden by the trees."

All the next day, Polly and Rowanna looked for the man to come walking across the fields. "He's a country boy, he'll find his way," Polly allowed. "He probably left before daylight."

But daughter Rowanna added, "I thought he might come by to bring back the quilt."

Polly replied, "He'll probably need it again. He's welcome to it. I only pray that he gets home safely."

Months later, Rowanna convinced her sister Nan and an older male friend to enter

Rowanna Kinkead

Nan Kinkead at age 19

Detail of The Cave Hill Farm Quilt showing some of the damage caused by the covering's long stay in the cave.

the cave, but they only found the lantern. That was proof that the young man had spent the night, but where was the quilt?

Long after the war had ended, two young boys asked permission to enter the cave. They took the same lantern Polly had given to the soldier. Inside, the two crawled toward a tiny hole where light from the outside streaked through. On an outcropping near the hole, they spied a white bundle. The boys removed it from the cave and returned to the Kinkeads to show them their treasure.

"The boys found the quilt!" Rowanna called to her mother.

They spread the wet quilt out on the grass. When Polly saw it, she said, "The soldier boy didn't take the quilt after all." When they hung the quilt on a line to dry, the damage caused by its stay in the cave became evident: broken stitches, frayed cloth, and cotton batting in damp, smelly wads.

Nan's feelings tempered as the war wore on and news of wounded and dead friends filtered back to the family. Nan secretly yearned for news of her boyfriend, Jim Whitney, who ministered to the sick and wounded of General Sherman's army as it swept south through Tennessee, Georgia, and finally South Carolina. Unfortunately, Jim never returned home.

After the war, without any news of Jim's fate, a friend of Nan's wrote to the army in Washington, D.C., seeking to obtain information about the young man. The friend eventually traveled to Jim's last known encampment in South Carolina, where he found a storekeeper who had buried several young soldiers and their doctor, Jim Whitney, who had contracted malaria from his patients and died. The storekeeper found the grave sites, but the handmade crosses had been toppled and the graves had been disturbed. The men's bodies were missing.

Although heartbroken, Nan was glad to know the full story. Among Jim's effects held by the army was an envelope containing her engagement ring. Nan married and had children of her own. She often told these stories to her granddaughter, who passed them on to her children and grandchildren. In 1986, at the age of eighty-three, Margaret Lyons Smith wrote a book about her grandmother's life, *Miss Nan Beloved Rebel*.

Irish Chain Flag Quilt

Displaying allegiance to one side or the other during the Civil War often meant trouble for families living in contested areas. Curtis McDowell of Sparta, Tennessee, in the foothills of the Cumberland Mountains east of Nashville, owned and operated the Cumberland Institute, a boarding school for boys and girls from the area. His wife, Margaret, had died in 1848, leaving Curtis with four children to raise: two teenage sons, Lafayette and Jackson, and two younger daughters, Amanda and Mary. Each of his children taught at the school prior to the war.

When the war began, McDowell, a Union sympathizer, found himself and his family in a precarious situation. A majority of Tennesseans had finally voted to secede, despite strong sentiment throughout the state for the North. McDowell's sons, when faced with the decision of which side to support, chose opposite paths. Lafayette joined a Confederate contingent and fought in many battles not far from his home. Jackson went to work for a small company in nearby Cookeville that published pro-Union broadsides and newsletters. Both sons remained close to the family, and neither was criticized for his choice.

Early in the war, with McDowell and his daughters trying their best to keep the school open, the family proudly flew the Stars and Stripes over the school's main building. One evening two Confederate soldiers rode up to the front gate of the McDowells' house on the hill. Amanda and Mary were home alone, and when the men reached the porch, Amanda opened the door.

"Is McDowell here?" one of the Confederates inquired. The girls noticed he held the wadded-up flag from the schoolhouse in his fist—the flag Amanda had so carefully made when the debating societies requested it.

Amanda and Mary McDowell, makers
Sparta, White County, Tennessee
c. 1862
Cotton fabric; pieced work
82″ x 70″
Betty McDowell, owner

"He is not here," Amanda said calmly, but her hand reached toward the latch of the door.

"Well, we can leave this—and our message— here!" said the leader as he tore the flag across and threw it to the ground, where he and the other soldier trampled it beneath their boots. "Tell McDowell that is the way we feel about his flag, and he had better keep it down."

The girls had learned early in the "disturbance" to say as little as possible, so they made no reply but stepped back enough to close the door and slide the heavy latch into place. They heard the men remount their horses and ride toward the valley with a great clatter and commotion.

A few minutes later, their father and some students returned. The girls felt great relief, for they feared that their father had been in the schoolhouse and would not have

McDowell family papers from the 1860s.

taken such an insult quietly. But he, too, had known what was best and had remained in one of the cabins until the soldiers had departed.

Sorrowfully, Amanda gathered up the torn flag and took it into the house. She stored it in a chest after cleaning off the muddy footprints and decided that she and Mary would one day make it into a quilt.

The one flag was actually used to make two Irish Chain quilts, which the sisters enjoyed displaying openly in their front parlor. Amanda's blue and white quilt has survived intact, having been handed down to the current generation by her descendants, but all that remains of Mary's red and white Irish Chain is a small segment.

Amanda McDowell kept a diary during the Civil War and also retained letters she received from her brothers. In her diary, Amanda reflected on such day-to-day concerns about life in wartime as making clothes for her soldier brother, the safety of her brother with Union sympathies, getting mail to and from her siblings, and worries about her father's health. She also reported on neighbors, newborn children, and a boyfriend for whom she secretly pined.

Notice advertising the Cumberland Institute.

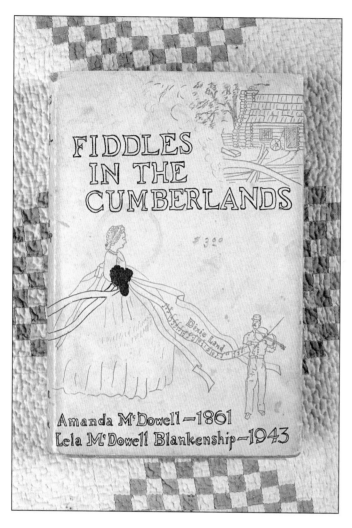

Fiddles in the Cumberlands *cover.*

In her book *Fiddles in the Cumberlands*, Lela McDowell Blankenship, Amanda's niece, wove a romantic account of Amanda's life that was based loosely on her diaries and papers, and included a story about the flag quilt. Jack and Betty McDowell recently re-issued the book, which was originally published in 1943 by Richard R. Smith, and have added information from the diaries and letters so that the account is more accurate.

The story of the red, white, and blue flag being preserved in two quilts is not related in Amanda's extant diaries, but it remains a part of the powerful oral history that, along with the quilts, has been passed down through generations of the McDowell family.

Crystal Springs Quilt

Elizabeth Armstrong Farmer was an exceedingly gracious wife who took pride in her well-appointed house in Floyd County, Georgia. The plantation land produced a bounty of food for the table as well as cotton, which provided a generous income as the family's major cash crop. When daughter Ellen announced her engagement to William Landers Selman, after he had gained the consent of her father, Joel Farmer, her parents arranged a festive and memorable wedding. The house was decorated with garden flowers and greens, the best linens and silver were laid out, and the guests celebrated the occasion with joyous enthusiasm. The year was 1857.

Within three short years, however, the war began and the happy life the Farmers had known changed quickly. Family members and acquaintances volunteered for the Confederate Army and were soon gone. In the ensuing months, groups of women gathered together to make uniforms and undergarments, prepare bandages, knit socks, and produce banners and flags. Elizabeth did her best to maintain a consistent routine and preserve what domestic tranquillity she could in spite of shortages of household supplies and a lack of help. Whatever spare moments she had were devoted to sewing and knitting for the Confederate cause.

In 1864 the Union Army was making a concerted effort to reach Atlanta. Battles were being fought throughout northern Georgia, and fearful residents took what precautions they could to preserve the safety of their families, homes, and possessions. The Northern campaign continued with a series of skirmishes, one of them within sight of the Farmers' house.

Throughout the South, families secured their treasures as best they could, but it took ingenuity to outsmart clever looters who knew that a patch of freshly turned earth might be a sign of buried goods. One soldier who investigated such a spot was rewarded with the body

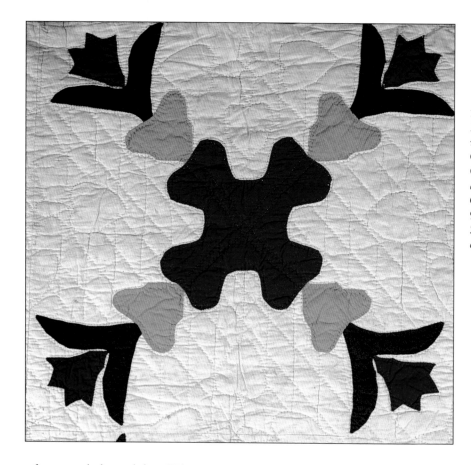

of a recently buried dog. Taking precautions against a raid, Elizabeth Farmer hid her best quilts in a trunk under some unfinished fancy work. Pressed for time, she wrapped the family silver in a tablecloth and lowered it down the well in a bucket.

As the fighting drew closer, Elizabeth went outside to watch from the porch. With a mixture of fear, anger, and loyalty, she paced back and forth shouting, "Hoorah for the Confederacy!" Her actions did not go unnoticed, and when the encounter was over, much of the property was destroyed and the silver was taken from the well. It did not pay to be such a vociferous Rebel, but it was the only way Elizabeth knew to fight back against the unfairness of war.

The quilts escaped notice by the Yankee soldiers and were saved. Later, when they were kept in Ellen Selman's cedar chest, Elizabeth's granddaughters hid apples between the quilts, a prank which always resulted in a scolding.

Narcissa's Quilt

A Southern plantation prior to the Civil War might consist of vast tracts of land cultivated by a hundred or more slaves to make it economically successful and support the owner's family in an agreeable style. More often, however, land holdings consisted of a few hundred acres, with only a few slaves who worked the land alongside their owners rather than under the watchful eye of an overseer or manager. Such was the plantation belonging to John and Narcissa Black of McNairy County in southwest Tennessee, bordering Mississippi.

John Black and Narcissa Erwin married in December 1836 and began to farm land next to his father's plantation. When John H. Black Sr. died in 1861, several of his slaves were inherited by his son, joining John's four. One was Chany Scot Black, a weaver. Narcissa, an expert seamstress, and Chany had a collaboration that lasted for ten years, even after Chany became a freedwoman.

Narcissa kept precise records of their work. Her diary covers the years during and after the war, and includes brief entries about the work she and Chany accomplished each day as well as other daily occurrences, major and

Homemade looms such as this were commonplace in Southern homes throughout the Civil War era.

FACING PAGE
Narcissa L. Erwin Black, maker
McNairy County, Tennessee
c. 1860
Cotton fabrics; reverse appliqué; quilted
76″ x 69″
Collection of the Old Capitol Museum of Mississippi History, Jackson; gift of Dr. and Mrs. Fayette Williams

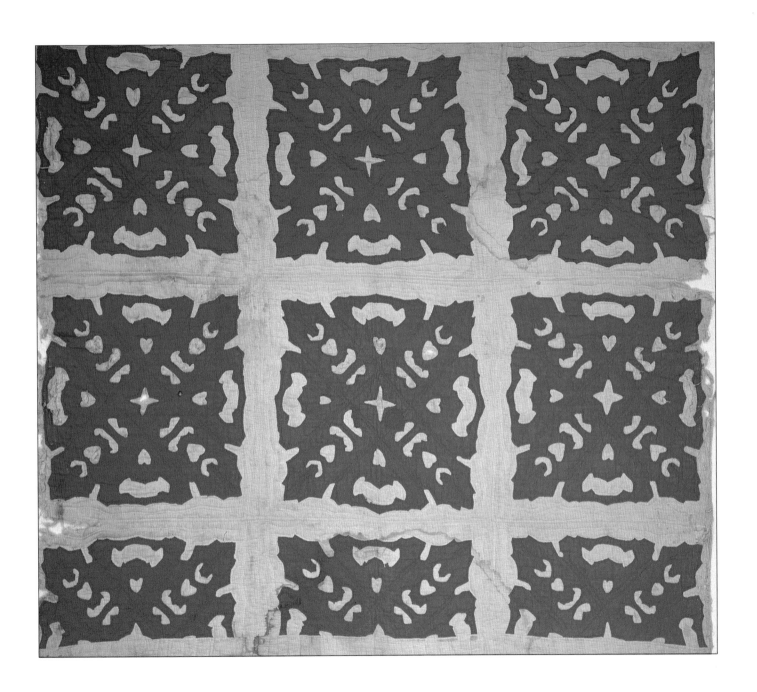

minor. Narcissa reported on the bloody battle of Shiloh in early April 1862, noting that "our house was croded [sic] with citizens and wounded men."

The area was devastated by heavy fighting, skirmishes, and raids on local citizens' property as Union forces prevailed, ultimately dooming the Confederates in the West. Not only were there appalling losses of military personnel and property, several of Narcissa's relatives and friends also were killed. The Black plantation was raided several times, and the appropriated items, including "one hundred bushels of corn and from eight hundred to one thousand Bundles fodder," were faithfully recorded in the diary. (In 1868 Narcissa applied for recompense from the United States government "for what the yankeys took from us" but got nothing.)

John Black was in declining health during the war years, and Narcissa, as head of the household, depended upon her production of textiles and clothing for income. She and Chany worked daily at the weaving, producing material for shirts, dresses, jeans, and coverlets, while Narcissa did the cutting and sewing, with only occasional access to a sewing machine.

The blockade imposed on the South created severe shortages of domestic supplies and fabric for housewives. When deliveries of cloth from New England mills and from Europe ceased, many women were obliged once again to produce handwoven material for clothing and household needs. Replacing silk finery with a homespun dress became a symbol of patriotism and loyalty to the Confederate cause. With the lack of available wearing apparel and linens, Narcissa and Chany's products were in great demand. As fast as Chany wove, Narcissa made the garments: pants, shirts, suspenders, dresses, sacques, riding skirts, aprons, bonnets, undergarments, and towels. Sometimes the payment was given in barter, trade, or other services instead of cash, as money, too, was in short supply.

Quilting was another activity mentioned in the diary. Two quilts were described as "fine" and one as a "corse quilt," perhaps made of the handwoven wartime linsey. Comforts—heavier bed quilts—were put in the quilt frame for tying or quilting. Occasionally, a quilting party for a house-raising took place.

Though fragile and worn, one of Narcissa Black's own quilts did last through the years. It has nine pieces of white background material on which are imposed red reverse-appliquéd cutwork designs. Undoubtedly, they were the invention of the maker as they have a very simple, naive quality.

With her husband's death in 1865, the end of the war, and the South's shattered economy, Narcissa found herself in financial difficulty. She disposed of household goods and tools at auction and eventually sold sections of the land she had inherited from her husband, while continuing to support herself by producing textiles. Chany, on the other hand, having saved all the money she had made apart from her required work, became economically independent after her emancipation. In succession, she purchased a cow, a horse, and a loom, and in 1870 built a house.

Narcissa remarried when she was sixty-seven and had a somewhat easier life. Chany moved away in 1872, but for ten years she and Narcissa had shared their daily work and supported each other emotionally and financially through the war years and afterward.

Colorful striped blankets and sheeting such as these exemplified Southern weaving during the 1860s.

Alabama Gunboat Quilt

Fundraising and soldiers' aid occupied many civilians during the War Between the States. In the North, well organized fairs were held to benefit the Sanitary Commission, the organization formed to provide medical care and personal comforts for Union soldiers. Individuals and groups made supplies for hospitals and rolled bandages, stitched uniforms and apparel, and gathered quilts and blankets, conscientiously meeting the requests from commission committees.

The support system in the Confederacy, while much less structured than that in the North, made the same efforts to meet the need for

LEFT AND DETAIL ON FACING PAGE
Martha Jane Hatter, maker
Greensboro, Hale County, Alabama
c. 1861
Silk taffeta, wool challis, and cotton fabrics;
appliqué; silk embroidery; stuffing
66˝ x 66˝
Collection of the Birmingham Museum of
Art, Birmingham, Alabama; museum
purchase with partial funds from the
Quilt Conservancy

critical supplies and assistance. Diary entries frequently refer to gatherings for quiltmaking and comfort-tying, sewing, and knitting.

Myra Inman Carter, a sixteen-year-old girl in Cleveland, Tennessee, noted each day's events as her life changed from one of ease and comfort to one of hard work.

> JULY 29, 1861 – Mother and Mrs. Cash went around to get the ladies to knit socks for the soldiers.
>
> AUG. 1, 1861 – Florence Johnson & Mrs. Montgomery were here to get blankets for the wounded volunteers.
>
> MAR. 12, 1862 – Mother went over to the "Soldier's Aid Society" this eve. Thinking of having a hospital here. We are going to tack comforts for them, poor fellows. Would that we had already gained our independence! and they could return home.

Diarist Mary Chesnut refers to various groups of women who sent donations of hospital supplies to Richmond in the early stages of the war. A heated discussion—"shrill and long and loud it was"—occurred when someone proposed that the supplies be shared with wounded and sick Yankee prisoners as well as with the Confederates who were hospitalized. Groups also met to make fundraising quilts, sell subscriptions to benefit the cause, and then offer the quilts for sale at auction to the highest bidder. Other items, such as jewelry, silver, china, art objects, and household goods, were donated for auction as well. Many family treasures were given up "for the cause" and never reached later generations.

Women in several Southern states formed societies to raise money specifically for the purchase of gunboats to defend coastal towns. In South Carolina, one woman noted in her diary that she had donated a string of pearls to a gunboat fair that raised a total of $2,000 for defense. Activities were highly competitive from group to group and from state to state. In 1862, Alabama newspapers published articles encouraging support of these local fundraising efforts. Patriotic participants bid in spirited rivalry on the goods donated for auction.

Martha Jane Hatter of Greensboro, Alabama, contributed two magnificent quilts worked with floral design in appliqué and embroidery. One of the quilts was "purchased" and then returned for resale four times, while the second was "sold" twice and then given back to Mrs. Hatter. The twice-sold quilt remained in her family until 1985, when it was acquired by the Birmingham Museum of Art.

Confederate naval forces sustained heavy losses in the spring of 1862, and enthusiasm for the gunboat campaign declined sharply. The goal of $80,000, the cost of a gunboat, was never realized, and the sum of approximately $4,000 that the campaign had raised was used to purchase hospital supplies instead.

The other quilts made by Mrs. Hatter also survived the war. The Gunboat Quilt-B, measuring 71″ x 68″, features a large embroidered basket in its center surrounded by a floral wreath. Twenty-one bouquets, appliquéd, stuffed, and embroidered, form the quilt's edge. The second quilt, a crib quilt measuring 37″ x 31 1/2″, has a center basket of flowers cut from printed floral chintz, appliquéd and embroidered, surrounded by a floral wreath, with lace at the outer edge of the quilt. Both quilts are in the collection of the First White House of the Confederacy in Montgomery, Alabama.

Quilts were among items sold at auction by Southern women's groups to raise money for Confederate gunboats, such as the C.S.S. Georgia, as seen in this 1863 engraving.

Basket Quilt

Mary High (1840–1931), like her counterpart Nan Kinkead in East Tennessee, was a staunch supporter of the secessionist cause. Mary lived in Middle Tennessee, which was occupied by Union forces in early 1862 following Confederate defeats at Fort Donelson and Shiloh in West Tennessee.

Mary High was twenty-two and betrothed to marry, but those were not marrying times. Mary and her fiancé were spies for the Confederacy. Her job was to transport messages behind the Union lines. According

FACING PAGE
Mary High Prince and friends, makers
Raus, Bedford County, Tennessee
1863-1864
Cotton fabric; pieced work
96″ x 74″
Emeline Prince Gist, owner

The Seventeenth Tennessee Infantry was on hand at Appomattox Court House, Virginia, April 9, 1865, when Gen. Robert E. Lee surrendered the Army of Northern Virginia to Union Gen. Ulysses S. Grant in the parlor of the Wilmer McLean house. [Surrender at Appomattox © Tom Lovell. Courtesy of The Greenwich Workshop, Inc., Shelton, Connecticut.]

Detail of Basket Quilt.

to her family, one particularly harrowing experience occurred when Mary was carrying a message to Columbia, Tennessee, and was apprehended in nearby Pulaski. The Union soldiers brought her to their camp to face their commanding officer. Left alone just a few moments, Mary quickly backed up to the fire and dropped the folded paper into the flames, which consumed the precious message. Without sufficient evidence to hold her, the Union commander released Mary and sent her home.

Her fiancé was not so lucky; he was hanged in Murfreesboro, Tennessee, for his spying activities. Mary and her fiancé's sister hitched horses to the family wagon and went to Murfreesboro to retrieve his body for burial back home.

As the war wore on, Mary High helped make this Basket Quilt, which bears the names of people from her hometown, the Raus community, as well as soldiers serving in the Seventeenth Tennessee Infantry Regiment. The Basket Quilt was raffled during the war to raise funds for the Confederate cause.

"Miss M. C. High," inscribed in ink, appears on the quilt, as does the name of the man Mary High eventually married, Benjamin P. Prince. Prince was known as a "rebel to the end" because when Gen. Robert E. Lee surrendered his forces at Appomattox Court House, Virginia, on April 9, 1865, the Tennessee Seventeenth Infantry was there. Those who stayed for the formal surrender were provided with mules for the trip home. Benjamin Prince and five other men from the Seventeenth chose not to surrender formally and walked all the way home. It took them several weeks. Furthermore, attempts in later years to convince this band of rebels to sign a pledge of allegiance to the Union were met with defeat.

Mary Prince's strong feelings lingered long after the war's end. She made the commemorative pillow on page 38.

Roses and Plumes Quilt

Mary Earl Underwood moved with her parents from South Carolina to north Georgia before the Civil War and enjoyed the pleasant life of a marriageable young woman. After becoming engaged, her fiancé, Captain J. Y. Wood, soon departed for service in the Confederate Army. Once, while home on leave, the captain brought Mary Earl a gift of several yards of fine linen fabric, which was becoming exceedingly scarce. She used the linen as background for an appliqué quilt of roses and plumes, a project that admirably filled the hours of her long wait. Mary Earl told her granddaughter in later years that when she became tired, her house girl would rub her arms and shoulders so that she could continue sewing. The quilt top was finished, the captain returned to wed Mary Earl, and the couple eventually had six children. Oddly enough, the quilt that Mary Earl had labored over for so many wearisome hours was never quilted.

Scarcely a home in the South was not affected in some way by the war. Men and boys volunteered for military service to seek adventure or because they felt a sense of duty or loyalty to the Confederate cause and whatever it represented to them. Few able-bodied men

For many Southern men and boys, military service during the war offered an unprecedented opportunity for adventure.

FACING PAGE
Mary Earl Underwood Wood, maker
Kensington, Georgia, 1861-1865
Cotton fabric on linen; appliqué; unquilted top
101˝ x 101˝
Collection of the Hunter Museum of American Art, Chattanooga, Tennessee; gift of Mary Lou Kell Camp

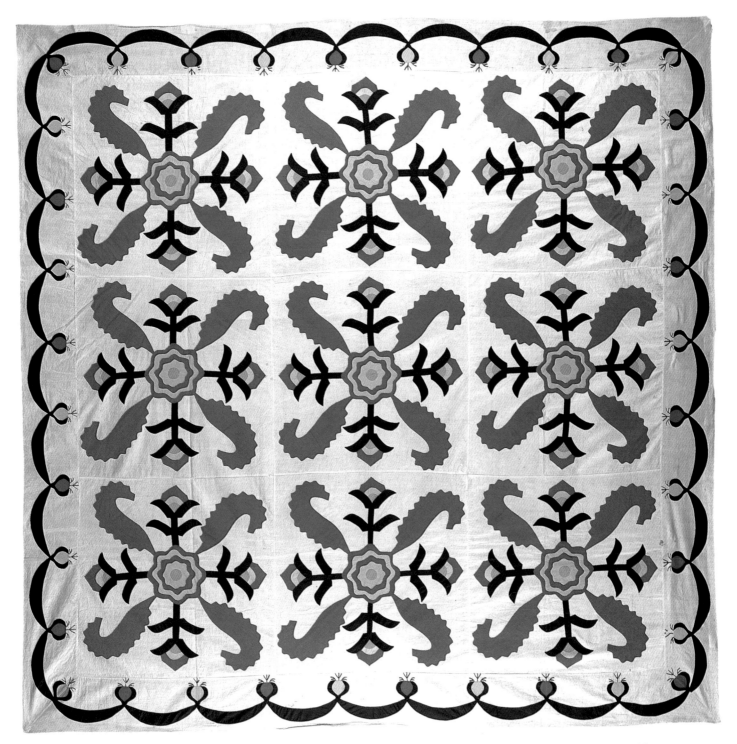

Detail of Roses and Plumes Quilt.

96   Southern Quilts

remained at home to continue agricultural activities and conduct business, and those who did were likely to be scorned for their lack of patriotism.

Each household bustled with excitement as preparations were made to send the volunteer soldiers off to war. The mother would scurry about, gathering articles she deemed necessary for her son's health and welfare—knitted socks, blankets and quilts for a bedroll, a few personal items—while tending to any last-minute sewing of underclothes and uniforms. A young daughter might assist her mother in the ritual and would always remember that day in future years.

Apprehension and sadness filled the hearts of those who said good-bye to their departing sons, husbands, and fathers. There was always fear that the men might never return.

Women did their best to persevere in the face of war's adversity, performing unaccustomed farm chores, spinning thread, weaving cloth, and scrimping and saving to buy food and basic necessities. More than one bride wore a gown made from curtain material at her hastily arranged wedding, and mothers wept through the night when there were no gifts for the children on Christmas morning.

The war dragged on, and many on the home front heard only rumors and fragments of news, more often bad than good. The answers to questions Southern families asked about their loved ones were often written in blood, in illness, loss of limb, wounds, despair, and death. Month after month, hearts were broken, dreams were shattered, and for many, life was never the same again.

Confederate Cradle Quilt

Many women have acknowledged quilting as the one thing that brought them through difficult times. After the death of a husband or child, their grief was measured in the quiet rhythm of the stitches. The process was the "something" needed to occupy the mind and lessen the pain.

During the Civil War years, quilting took on a new meaning as it offered a distraction from the clouds of anxiety that covered the land. Long hours spent waiting for news passed more quickly when the hands had something to do. One woman wrote a letter to her husband in the army describing her daily activities and saying that her "tasks drove dull care away." Through concentration on her work she gained some

Jefferson Finis Davis and Varina Howell Davis, the future president and first lady of the Confederacy, c. 1849. The couple married in 1845, the same year Davis went to Washington as a Mississippi congressman. Davis served with distinction in the Mexican War and as U.S. secretary of war, but just three months after Lincoln's election, he was inaugurated as president of the Confederate States of America.

Mrs. Robert E. Lee, Mrs. Jefferson Davis, Miss Maggie Davis, Mrs. Henry Foote, Miss Margaret Howell, and Miss Rachel
Seay, makers
Richmond, Virginia
1863
Red and white silk, black velvet; template-pieced work
48″ x 35 ¹/₄″
Property of the Carter House Association, Inc., Franklin, Tennessee; gift of Mrs. Thomas Edward Brune and Col. W. S. Tyson

When the Confederacy's capital was moved to Richmond, Virginia, Varina Davis was chastised by the city's social mavens for a host of perceived shortcomings, but almost no one questioned her dedication to her husband and family.

contentment, some relief from the nagging thoughts of her husband's vulnerability at the battlefront.

Spinning, weaving, quilting, the remodeling of clothes, and other efforts to improvise became increasingly difficult as the war ground on. Silk dresses were cut up for handkerchiefs. Carpets became bedcovers. Old garments gained new life with color from the dye pot. Women vied with each other in searching for clever ways to circumvent shortages and create acceptable substitutes.

Even the wives of high-ranking officials and military leaders of the Confederacy had to learn new patterns of life. They attempted to maintain as normal a routine as possible, nurture their children, and provide their husbands with the appropriate settings for their careers in spite of the turbulent times. Woven into the tapestry of the women's lives were the stresses of the war, the uncertainties of military action, and the constant bickering among the Southern political leaders. In Richmond, Virginia, and Charleston, South Carolina, social activities continued, but in a less lavish manner. Dinner-party menus depended upon the availability of meat, produce, and spirits. Like women in other Southern cities and on farms and plantations, the women of Richmond volunteered their services to make clothing as well as supplies for military and hospital use. They cared for the sick and wounded. They knitted and they sewed.

Mary Chesnut described a visit on February 26, 1864, to Mrs. Robert E. Lee in Richmond: Then paid our respects to Mrs. Lee. Her room was like an industrial school—everybody so busy. Her daughters were all there, plying their needles, and several other ladies. . . . When we came out: "Did you see how the Lees spend their time! What a rebuke to the taffy parties!" [Mary Chesnut was giving taffy parties for the young ladies who were staying with her as entertainment for their admirers.]

At other times the sewing was done more for

Gen. Robert Edward Lee and wife, the former Mary Anna Randolph Custis, c. 1865. One of the Civil War's most inspirational military leaders, Lee compiled an unrivaled military record and, according to many historians, held off Southern defeat for years. The couple had four daughters and three sons, and made their permanent home at Arlington, in Virginia, one of several estates inherited by Mary, the great-granddaughter of Martha Washington.

pleasure. Imagine Mrs. Jefferson Davis, Mrs. Robert E. Lee, and their friends gathered in the parlor for an afternoon of socializing. Even though Senator Henry S. Foote was a harsh critic of President Davis, Mrs. Foote and Mrs. Davis did not embrace their husbands' differences. One can imagine the women as they sat together and chatted while stitching on blocks for a small quilt of white silk stars with black velvet centers, set with red silk pieces. Were the silks formerly elegant dresses belonging to one of the ladies? Was the velvet material taken from a worn cloak? What was the conversation that day? For whom was the quilt being made? How satisfying it would be to have the answers!

Many of those questions remain unanswered, but there may be a clue to the selection of the pattern for the crib quilt. Mrs. Jane Weaver, an editor for the popular *Peterson's Magazine*, published a pattern for a bed quilt in her column in April 1859. She wrote: "a bed quilt . . . which needs no description, and which we have designed ourself." The needlework authors frequently borrowed designs from other publications prior to the enactment of copyright laws, and many of them were not acquainted with handwork or quilt construction themselves. Mrs. Weaver's design appears to be an assemblage of several parts and not typical of a quiltmaker's quilt. No explanation or pattern accompanies the quilt, but its center could well be the source of design for the Confederate Cradle Quilt.

Whig's Defeat Quilt

Charles Screven Gaulden was born in 1812 in Liberty County, Georgia, not far from Savannah, and after completing his studies at the University of Georgia, was admitted to the bar. With a sense of adventure, he moved to the extreme western portion of the state, where he practiced law and acquired considerable wealth. In 1859 Gaulden decided to move his family to Brooks County, in the southernmost part of Georgia. He established a large plantation, Okapilco, where his wife and seven children enjoyed the prosperity of a thriving planter's community.

At all times and in all seasons, work was being done to maintain Gaulden's large family and the slaves who labored in the fields and assisted with household duties. While many furnishings and necessities were ordered from Savannah, some things were made on the estate, including furniture for the extended family. An itinerant cabinetmaker scheduled regular visits to Okapilco when he was in the vicinity. Charles's wife, Charlotte, was especially proud of the handsome four-poster bed the man had crafted from plantation timber and was not content until, assisted by members of her household, she had made an intricate pieced quilt to adorn it. As unmarried Charlotte LeSueur, she had acquired fine needlework skills in her French Huguenot family, and she continued to enjoy sewing throughout her life.

The plantation was always bustling with such activities as planting or harvesting, kitchen-gardening, butchering, weaving, sewing, and quilting. Visitors came and went, and parties and church programs added variety to the days. But the good times were not to last. The Civil War affected the Gaulden plantation as it did almost every other homestead in the South as its men and boys reacted quickly to the call to military service.

Charlotte's brother, Thomas LeSueur, volunteered immediately for the

FACING PAGE AND DETAIL ABOVE
Charlotte LeSueur Gaulden, maker
Brooks County, Georgia
c. 1860
Cotton fabrics; pieced work
100″ x 99″
Collection of the McMinn County Living Heritage Museum, Athens; gift of Gay McNemer, great-
great-granddaughter of the quiltmaker

Confederate Army and headed east, where he fought in the campaign to hold and defend Virginia. Wounded, he was taken prisoner and sent to a detention camp. Concerned about Thomas's condition, the Gauldens sent a trusted slave named Captain to care for him, but Charlotte's brother succumbed to his wounds and the illness that accompanied them. Captain lovingly placed Thomas LeSueur's body in a casket and brought it back to Okapilco for burial.

It was a sad homecoming, for instead of being able to nurse her brother back to health in her cheerful bedroom and smoothing her prized quilt over him, Charlotte had to prepare Thomas's funeral. The family and friends gathered at the Baptist church for hymns and scripture readings and then watched as the casket was lowered into the ground at the family cemetery. The marker reads:

Thomas LeSueur
Volunteer Soldier
CSA

HIDING THE TREASURES

George Washington Gordon Quilt

Residents of Middle Tennessee were more than a little concerned for the safety of their homes as the Northern army moved through the state. How best to secure the most valuable possessions was on every housewife's mind. Numerous stories of prized treasures buried in family quilts are undoubtedly true.

George Washington Gordon and his family lived comfortably in their gracious home, Boxwood, in Columbia, forty miles south of Nashville. Frequent visits by relatives and friends provided occasions for parties and elegant dining. The finest table setting for honored guests included two decanters and dozens of glasses, in three sizes, of beautiful Bohemian handblown crystal.

Threatened by the likelihood of marauding troops, the family wrapped the glassware in old newspapers and placed it in a wicker champagne basket, which was stored carefully in the attic along with a favorite chintz-appliquéd friendship quilt and other

DETAIL AND FACING PAGE
Forty-eight guests of Gordon Springs Resort, makers
Catoosa County, Georgia
1854-1856
White cotton; assorted glazed chintz; appliqué
106″x 108″
Collection of the Atlanta History Center, Atlanta, Georgia; gift of Diana Stimson Webb, Mary Stimson Haskins, Marshall Stimson II, and other descendants of George Washington Gordon

articles. Shortly thereafter, G. W. Gordon volunteered for the Confederate Army and left for the war, never to return. Life at Boxwood continued, but the carefree gaiety it had known before the conflict was gone forever.

Members and descendants of the Gordon family continued to reside in the house until the late 1940s, when it was offered for sale. Only then, as the contents were being prepared for distribution among surviving relatives, were the Bohemian glass—still wrapped in newspapers from 1861—and the friendship quilt brought down from the attic. Both were acquired by Mary Gordon Stimson, granddaughter of G. W. Gordon, the original recipient of the quilt.

Detail of George Washington Gordon Quilt.

The quilt had been made during the summers of 1854, 1855, and 1856 at Gordon Springs, near Dalton, Georgia. George Washington Gordon and his brother, the Rev. Zachariah Gordon, had established a summer resort at the springs that was a haven for residents of Memphis, Charleston, Savannah, and Macon seeking to escape the heat and epidemics that often plagued cities in the warmer months. Families, many of them related to the Gordons, gathered at the resort, and there was much fun and frolic, especially among the young people.

Needlework was favored by the ladies as a quiet pastime during the hot summer days. As a diversion, they enthusiastically accepted a proposal to make a chintz quilt for G. W. Gordon, who promised to host a gala ball for the women upon its completion. Background pieces of white cotton cloth were distributed to the participants, who cut floral designs from chintz fabric to appliqué onto the squares. New arrivals at the springs were recruited for the project. The completed blocks were signed, and some were dated, by forty-eight women from Alabama, Florida, Georgia, South Carolina, and Tennessee who took part in the work. It took three summers to finish all the blocks, which were finally assembled, and then the top, filler, and backing were put in a quilt frame for quilting.

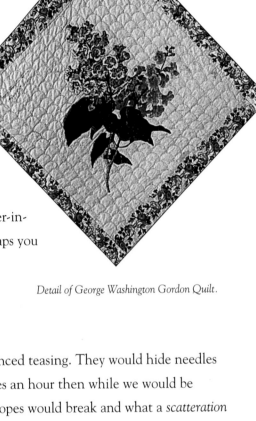

Detail of George Washington Gordon Quilt.

On September 30, 1856, Mary Brown Gordon, G. W. Gordon's eldest daughter, sent a description of the undertaking to her future sister-in-law, Annie LeConte, of Macon, Georgia: "Perhaps you would like to hear about the quilt. Well it is completed at last and really looks very pretty though we had a time of it the last two or three days it was in the frame. The gentlemen took a notion they must have their fun as they commenced teasing. They would hide needles and thread and make us look for them sometimes an hour then while we would be sitting around stitching away industriously the ropes would break and what a *scatteration* of thimbles thread and everything that happened to be on top. Thus matters went on until the ladies would stand it no longer so went in early one morning and finished before they came over but we did not have the promised party there were so few here."

The friendship quilt from Gordon Springs symbolizes the way of life in the antebellum South and, secure in the attic at Boxwood, escaped the ravages of war.

Pot of Flowers Quilt

Sitting on the front porch of her grandmother's house in 1962, eighteen-year-old Marilyn DeMarcus received a precious family bundle—a pillowcase containing a red and green appliqué quilt and a story about a female ancestor who concealed the quilt in a most ingenious way.

Unknown quiltmaker from Green family
Union County, Tennessee
1850s
Cotton fabric; appliqué
86˝ x 67˝
Marilyn DeMarcus Harmon, owner

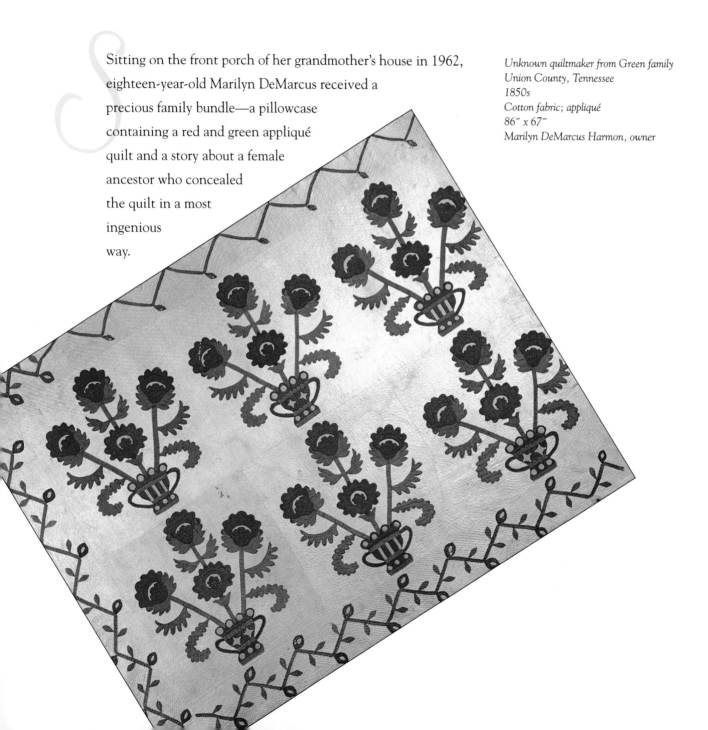

"At eighteen, I was not much interested in a quilt or family history, I am ashamed to say. I wish now that I had asked for more details. I think the maker was Granny Green, my great-great-great grandmother, but I am not even certain about the number of "greats.""

The quilt's survival story, as it relates to the Civil War, has been an enduring legacy for the family. It has been retold countless times and the details have remained unchanged: When threatened by the presence of troops in the vicinity of her home, the quiltmaker hid the quilt under her dress to appear pregnant. This, she hoped, would prevent Yankee soldiers from stealing it. At night, the quilt was placed in a hollow stump in the yard. The quilt survived and, with its story, has been handed down from generation to generation of the family.

Southern family histories abound with accounts of uninvited soldiers entering houses, front yards, and barns looking for bedding, valuables, and a dry place to sleep. Owners devised ingenious schemes to conceal their most precious goods. Most families in the counties of East Tennessee, where this quilt was made, voted against secession, and few were staunch supporters of either side of the conflict. However, the area became a major route for troops heading north and south, and soldiers often approached local families for food, clothing, and shelter. Rumors of widespread stealing and plundering heightened the sense of fear for loss of property among farmers and their families. People were angry, frightened, and apprehensive.

Margaret Stakely wrote to her sister Carrie on February 21, 1865, about a scary encounter she had at her parents' home in Madisonville, Tennessee: "We had a little excitement here last Sabbath and Monday. Some troops came in town and tore up things generally, ending with the threat to burn the town. On Sunday evening Ma was at Mrs. Coffin's and I was at home when two came into the yard and asked questions and then one of them entered the house & rummaged about a while, but took nothing but a quilt & a tooth brush. And he afterwards told in town that he would not have gone into the house if I had not talked 'so saucy' to him. I unfortunately used an expression which he construed to mean something very different from what I intended it

Detail of Pot of Flowers Quilt.

should. The quilt was one which Ma prized very highly, and if it were something of ours, or more value, I would not feel so badly about it, but I am sorry that she should lose anything through any wrong of mine."

Margaret's mother added a postscript to the letter: "Dear Carrie, I do not care at all for the quilt that was taken, nor do I have any idea it was taken on account of what M. said. It was providential hindrance."

Four long years of living under the watchful eye of soldiers had hardened Mother Stakely.

When Southern troops advanced on Knoxville, Tennessee, in November 1863, Northern cavalry under Brig. Gen. William Sanders delayed their advance, giving the Union occupation force time to strengthen its defenses. Sanders was mortally wounded, and nearby Fort Loudon was renamed Fort Sanders in his honor. Four Confederate attacks were thwarted before the Southern forces withdrew.

Pieced Rose Quilt

According to family history, this Pieced Rose quilt was buried with the family silver during the Civil War so that it would not be taken by soldiers. Why would this quilt have been valued as highly as the family silver? The red and green floral quilt with its exceptionally fine needlework and sophisticated design was destined to be a family heirloom. In the 1850s, this type of quilt was considered the epitome of quilt design and technical skill. It would be the masterpiece a quilter would undertake to prove her worth as a fine needlewoman.

Antebellum quilts in floral designs similar to the Pieced Rose were made as wedding gifts, tokens of friendship, and contest entries. Most were appliqué, but this particular rose block was pieced in pie-shaped segments, and the circular floral units seamed into the white foundation cloth. Embroidered details gave botanical realism to the rose design. This quilt was further enhanced by adding stuffing to the quilted undulating vines that cross the surface.

Jacquard-woven coverlets produced in the 1840s incorporated similar design plans: equal-sized floral blocks comprising a central field surrounded by a border with an undulating vine. At the edges of the field, half of the unit was used, and in the corners a quarter bloom was added to fill the background space. Quiltmakers in the 1850s may have mimicked these design choices in their appliqué quilts.

FACING PAGE
Mother of Hester Gregg Susong, maker
Greene County, Tennessee
1850s
Cotton fabric, pieced and embroidered
87″ x 68″
Kathryn Susong Neas, owner

Detail of Pieced Rose Quilt.

The Forest Home Quilt

Before the war, Lucy Virginia Smith French and her husband, John Hopkins French, had perfected the fine art of southern living at their extensive domain, Forest Home, near McMinnville, Tennessee. Their children were happy and healthy, their home was elegantly furnished, their land was productive, and the garden flourished under the careful tending of its mistress. While Virginia enjoyed success as a writer of novels, poems, and short stories, that was secondary to the devotion she had for her family, home, art, music, and flowers.

Prior to making a business trip to New Orleans, John was instructed to purchase a length of plum-colored silk for a quilt. Virginia painted flowers from her own garden to use for embroidery patterns and with colored threads created a handsome bedcover. John

Soldiers on both sides often resorted to foraging to supplement their rations. Authorized foraging parties generally issued receipts for provisions taken, but unofficial foragers frequently took what they could and sometimes brutalized civilians seeking to stop them.

Lucy Virginia Smith French, maker
McMinnville, Tennessee
c. 1858
Plum-colored silk satin; rose-colored silk backing; wool, silk, and cotton embroidery thread; appliqué
81 1/2″ x 72″
Collection of the Tennessee State Museum, Nashville; gift of Mrs. Henry B. Gilman Jr.

Detail of Forest Home Quilt.

was especially gratified that the quilt received two awards at an exhibition in 1859.

The peaceful tranquillity of Forest Home changed rapidly after the occupation of Nashville by the Union Army in 1862. The region was ravaged by Northern as well as Southern units as they repeatedly advanced and retreated through the area. Virginia wrote in her diary in August of that year: "Never shall I forget the scenes that occurred here . . . the meanest looking wretches I ever saw, racing to and fro, everywhere in search of food . . . digging potatoes, pulling corn, milking the cows . . . racing about the orchard shaking down half-ripe fruit with the fierceness of famine and the voracity of wild animals." And the next month: "Alas! our place shows what it is to live near the track of an army. Fences, gates . . . are no more, corn fields bare or trodden under foot— gardens and flowers withered and gone."

Bedding was immediately requisitioned by any passing troops, and the family's supply was reduced to the barest necessity. Virginia took up the family carpets to cut into covers for a nearby military camp and hospital, saving only the carpet in the front bedroom, "lest someone might be sick."

The prize-winning quilt was retained for that same bedroom, and on at least one occasion, when the homestead was being pillaged, Mrs. French placed the family silver under the silk quilt and feigned illness to successfully protect her possessions. The house was destroyed by fire after the war, but the silver and the quilt were saved.

As the war continued, Virginia wrote in her diary of the severe depression and physical illness that were brought on by the devastating experiences she endured. In May 1864 she wrote about setting out plants at Beersheba Springs, Tennessee, where she had gone to regain her health: "I am as fond of flowers as ever. . . . It is the one trait of civilization left after the hardening, barbarizing influence of the horrid war."

Virginia eventually regained her vitality, resumed her literary career, and became editor of *Southern Ladies Book*.

Turkey Tracks Quilt

Victoria Darwin Caldwell took great pride in her quilts and devoted lavish amounts of time, money, and attention to their making. Like many of her neighbors in Rhea County, she practiced stipple quilting in the background around the various motifs and placed additional stuffing into the quilted design to give it greater emphasis. She liked to add handmade fringe to the edge of the quilts in place of borders.

The joy Victoria experienced in running her household and creating a pleasant environment for her family ceased as the war came to Tennessee. Troops from both armies alternately swept across the land, and with few or no supplies to sustain them,

Quiltmaker Victoria Darwin Caldwell, at right with grandchild, is shown with her sister.

Detail of Turkey Tracks Quilt.

soldiers were compelled to forage for food and provisions. Crops were trampled, livestock was killed, storehouses were raided, and bedding was confiscated with no regard for the owners' hardships. Outwitting the marauders became a contest of cunning for those who refused to abandon their homes.

Victoria raised a portion of the flooring in her house and beneath it stored the family's most valuable possessions, including her quilts. The floor was replaced and the cache remained undetected during the conflict.

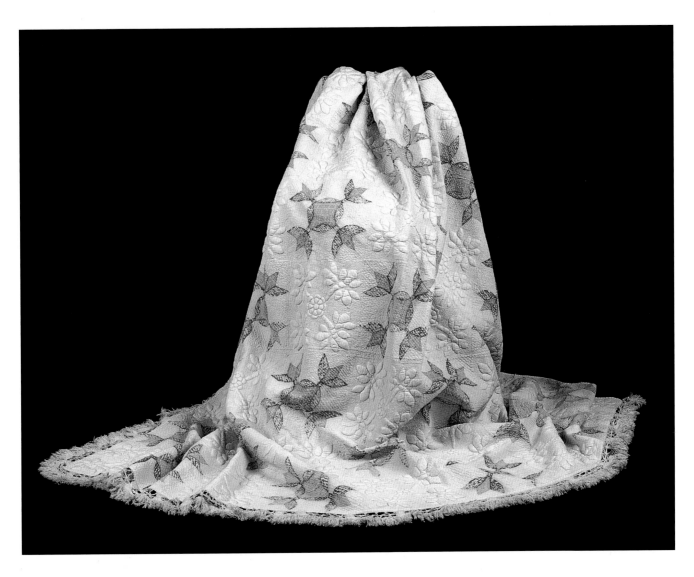

Victoria Darwin Caldwell, maker
Spring City, Rhea County, Tennessee
c. 1850-1860
Cotton fabric; pieced work
95″ x 85″
Mary Heiskell Wasson, owner

Cotton Boll Quilt

No television cameramen or war correspondents were present to provide hourly updates of military activity during the Civil War. News was more likely to be rumor than fact, and the accuracy of any report depended on the observer of the moment and the number of times the account was repeated. Obtaining a true assessment of conditions was difficult because of the fear and anxiety generated by each negative report.

When Gen. William Tecumseh Sherman was pushing through Georgia and South Carolina in 1864, word of his advance spread like wildfire. Southerners along any route Sherman might take were terrified as news of his exploits led them to expect severe pillaging and destruction. Word of his approach called for immediate action to protect one's treasures. Valuables were buried or hidden in dark attics, hollow logs, and caves. In order to ensure maximum security, residents sought hiding places that were unusual and inaccessible. Who knows whether all those valuables were ever found?

Temperance Neely Smoot was determined that her prized Cotton Boll quilt would not be snatched up by a Union soldier. She had labored too long over the appliqué work and the triple sashing with which to join the four large square blocks to see the quilt thrown on the ground and used as a bedroll. It had taken a long time to card the cotton filler and put in all the quilting stitches. The quilt and all the memories associated with it were too dear to Temperance, and she could not bear to see the work taken away.

Since it was known that Union troops had set fire to countless houses and barns during Sherman's March to the Sea and the campaign through South Carolina, it was prudent to choose a hiding place away from those structures. Temperance folded her quilt carefully and placed it in a trunk with other valuables. The trunk was then concealed in a nearby swamp. The valuables remained safe from looters, but the trunk developed a leak and the quilt was stained by water during a rainstorm. The two brown stains that remain as part of the quilt's history are emblems of strength and survival.

Temperance Neely Smoot, maker
Rowan County, North Carolina
c. 1860
Brown (originally red) and green cotton on white cotton fabric; appliqué
90˝ x 80˝
Pearl Turner Peebles, owner

Cockscomb and Currants Quilt

The reasons for secession varied from state to state and person to person. States along the southeastern coast and in the Deep South were more firmly united against the Union than were the border states of Tennessee and Kentucky. Although there was strong opposition to Abraham Lincoln and the Republican Party in Tennessee, the vote to leave the Union was soundly defeated—that is, until Lincoln, three months after his inauguration as president, issued a call for 75,000 volunteers to go to South Carolina and resolve the conflict, an action that caused a reversal in the Tennessee vote.

Throughout the war, Southerners' opinions differed on policy and military strategy. Even Jefferson Davis, president of the Confederacy, seemed to have as many detractors as he did admirers. The sharpest differences, though, occurred in families whose loyalties were divided between North and South.

DETAIL ABOVE AND FACING PAGE
Beulah Belle Poyner, maker
Paducah, Kentucky, or possibly made in Tennessee
c. 1860
Cotton fabric; appliqué; padded work
86˝ x 74˝
Mr. Hardin Pettit, owner

The resulting emotional conflict drove many relatives apart and shattered family unity.

Kentucky, the state in which both Lincoln and Davis were born, remained neutral, although it sent volunteers to both the Union and Confederate armies. During the Western Campaign, both armies moved back and forth across Kentucky. It was not necessary for residents to identify the troops since loyalty made little difference when protecting one's property. Both sides raided the countryside at will, and guerrilla bands took advantage of the chaos to rob and kill.

Mrs. M. E. Poyner of Paducah, Kentucky, finished making a quilt shortly before the war. She had undertaken the difficult task of appliquéing cockscombs and roses, adding dozens of stuffed currants, and had finished the edge with a precisely applied piped binding to add even more elegance to the quilt. Mrs. Poyner had no intention of letting a soldier carry her precious quilt away, so she hid it in a sugar chest whenever troops moved into the area. Loyalty to the Confederate cause or to the Union meant nothing. War was war.

Beulah Belle Poyner's beautiful quilt was saved from destruction during the war, but that was not the only time it was spared. In the early twentieth century the quilt was being exhibited at a fair in Paducah when a heavy thunderstorm destroyed the building's roof. The owner rushed to the fairgrounds, rescued her quilt, and took it home to dry. A water stain is still visible to record that part of the quilt's history. Several decades later, during the flood of 1937, valuables were moved to the second floor of the family's house to escape water damage. "When the lady got in the boat to leave, she had the quilt in her arms," says its owner. It is a quilt that has led a charmed life.

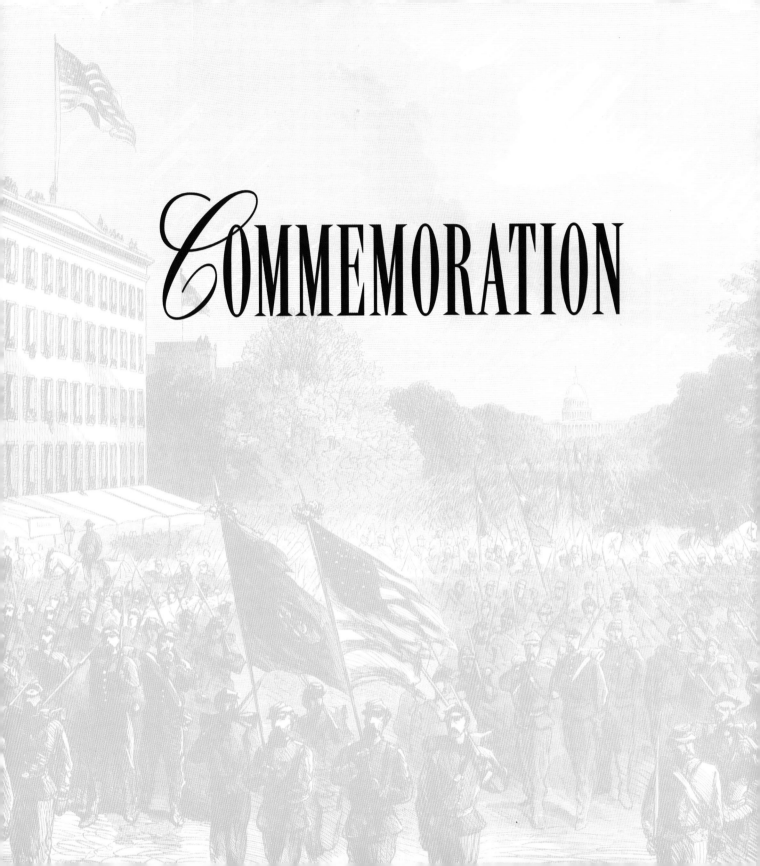

COMMEMORATION

Confederate Rose Quilt

James Marcus de LaFayette Nunnelee, who preferred to be called "Mark," was a surveyor by trade. Prior to the war, Mark used his drafting skills to design this original rose design. His wife and three teenage daughters did the piecing, appliqué, and quilting. The two oldest daughters, Sally and Mary, had learned the requisite needlework skills at a female academy in Columbia, Tennessee.

When the Civil War broke out, Mark Nunnelee, at the age of thirty-four and with six young children to support, joined the Confederate Army and later rose to the rank of captain. He was never well after the war, living just nine more years and dying at the age of fifty.

The quilt was used often on one of the family beds during the war and was known ever after as the family's Confederate Rose Quilt. In 1966, on the occasion of her ninety-ninth birthday, Carrie Nunnelee Heath, another daughter of Mark and Lucy Nunnelee, bequeathed two family quilts to the Tennessee State Museum: Confederate Rose and Tennessee Sunburst.

FACING PAGE
James Marcus de LaFayette Nunnelee, his wife, Lucy Jane Fowlkes Nunnelee, and three eldest daughters, Sally, Mary, and Martha Eveline, makers
Centerville, Hickman County, Tennessee
1850s
Cotton fabric; pieced work and appliqué
89˝ x 88˝
Collection of the Tennessee State Museum, Nashville; gift of Louise Nunnelee Snider

The Blue and the Gray Log Cabin Quilt

Although Illinois was a Northern state and the home of Abraham Lincoln, the Great Emancipator, the Mason-Dixon line extended across the state's mid-point. As southern Illinois counties along the Ohio and Mississippi Rivers are closer to Memphis and Nashville than to Chicago, and many families living there had migrated from Tennessee and Kentucky, their sympathies for the Southern cause were naturally strong.

Little is known of the political beliefs of the Leys family of Anna, Illinois, where this quilt was made and preserved, or whether family members living in the South actually wore Confederate gray. When the quilt was purchased in 1973, the family was reluctant to talk about the quilt's history.

The lack of information created a mystery the new owner wanted to unravel. Her search for information led her on a journey to Anna to interview descendants of the Leys family and make inquiries at the local historical society. She eventually consulted staff members at museums and libraries.

People in Anna, Illinois, who knew the Leys were not forthcoming with facts about the quilt or the family. The quilt's owner learned from an elderly man that the town had been a stopping place on the Underground Railroad but also that many of the townspeople had been "strong for the South." This may have been the reason family members did not want to discuss the quilt. Being a Confederate sympathizer in the Land of Lincoln was something one did not discuss even 100 years after the fact.

In order to date the quilt, the owner turned

FACING PAGE
Member of the Leys family, maker
Anna, Union County, Illinois
c. 1900
Wool, cotton, taffeta, silk fabrics; foundation-pieced
69" x 63"
Judith Trager, owner

Detail of The Blue and the Gray Log Cabin Quilt.

her attention to clues in the various fabric pieces. She believed the type of fabric, the dyes, and the woven structure might date the fabrics and therefore the quilt. In 1976, while at the Smithsonian's Museum of American History, Judith Trager asked to examine Civil War uniforms. The curator showed her both Union and Confederate examples. The tightly woven blue-rich purple wool fabric of the Union uniform contrasted with the lighter weight, more loosely woven gray fabric of the Confederate examples. Examples of both the blue and gray wool can be seen in the Leys Family Log Cabin quilt.

Judith Trager believes the quilt was made about 1900 from remnants of Union and Confederate uniforms. The backing was probably added sometime during the 1920s. Perhaps, she surmised, Mrs. Leys had sons who served on opposite sides of the conflict. Many women in southern Illinois, southern Ohio, and southern Indiana did.

RECONSTRUCTION

Rocky Mountain Quilt

Middle Tennessee saw heavy fighting during the war, with first one side and then the other gaining the advantage. Day after day, residents could hear the sound of guns and cannon, yet they tried to maintain as much normalcy in their lives as possible despite the military activity nearby. Martha Jane Edwards and her sixteen-year-old daughter, Mary Lavinia, tried to perform the usual chores around the homestead in the absence of their menfolk, who were at war. Life was not easy, and they were often discouraged by their inability to keep up the work, a task that was made more difficult by the anxiety they felt for their loved ones. In February 1862 Nashville was abandoned by the Confederates and occupied by Northern forces. On December 26 of that year, to secure their supply lines to Tennessee's capital city, Union troops left Nashville and advanced on Southern units massed near Murfreesboro, some thirty miles southeast. After several skirmishes between the opposing forces, the Confederates attacked on December 31 and surprised the Northerners, forcing them to retreat. But three days later, after both sides had sustained heavy casualties in what became known as the battle of Stones River, the Confederates withdrew south toward Shelbyville and Union troops occupied Murfreesboro.

Through unknown circumstances, a Yankee soldier who had been wounded in a skirmish at Hoover's Gap was received into the Edwardses' home, located several miles southwest of Hoover's Gap in the rural community of Fosterville. While the battle of Stones River raged, the soldier was hidden in the attic, where he was fed and nursed back to health by Mrs. Edwards and her daughter. Even though they were staunch Rebel supporters and had menfolk in the Confederate Army,

FACING PAGE
Makers unknown
New York State
After 1863
Cotton fabric; pieced work
88" x 73"
Jeanne Gilmore Webb, owner

Detail of Rocky Mountain Quilt.

140   *Southern Quilts*

they felt it was their Christian duty to care for the enemy soldier. For long afterward, the man's bloodstains remained visible in the attic.

When his wounds had healed and he had regained his strength, the soldier returned to his home state of New York. In gratitude for the "southern hospitality" the man had received, the man's family members made this Rocky Mountain quilt as a gift for the Edwardses. Years later, Mary Lavinia Gilmore told the story to her granddaughter, Jeanne Gilmore Webb.

In the nineteenth century this pattern was known as Rocky Mountain or Rocky Mountain Road, but it has come to be known as New York Beauty after the Stearns & Foster Company published it with their Mountain Mist patterns under that name in 1930.

One of the bloodiest engagements of the war, the battle of Stones River left homes and other structures in nearby Murfreesboro, Tennessee, crowded with wounded as nearly one-fourth of all combatants became casualties. After three days of fighting, Southern troops withdrew from the battlefield on the morning of January 3, 1863, leaving the Union to proclaim victory.

Feed the Hungry Quilt

The men had gone to war. No one remained to plant and harvest the crops or manage the few animals that were left after the army had taken the horses and mules. Food and household goods were in short supply. Confederate money was almost worthless. Mothers cut up their own dresses to make clothing for their daughters, and their sons wore jeans made from handwoven linsey. Children went barefoot most of the time because there were no shoes. Then, word would come that the husband had been killed at Wilson's Creek or in some other battle. A few neighbors would share some of their own scant supplies to help the family through the worst times. The prevailing mood was one of utter despair, and the future appeared dismal, with little prospect of happiness.

Virtually no able-bodied Southern men remained at home once the war was in full swing, which made life quite difficult for the women, children, and elderly who stayed behind.

FACING PAGE
Women of the Methodist-Episcopal Church, South, makers
Lexington, Missouri
c. 1866
Silk fabric; pieced work; sequin embroidery
80″ x 74″
Collection of the Missouri Historical Society, St. Louis

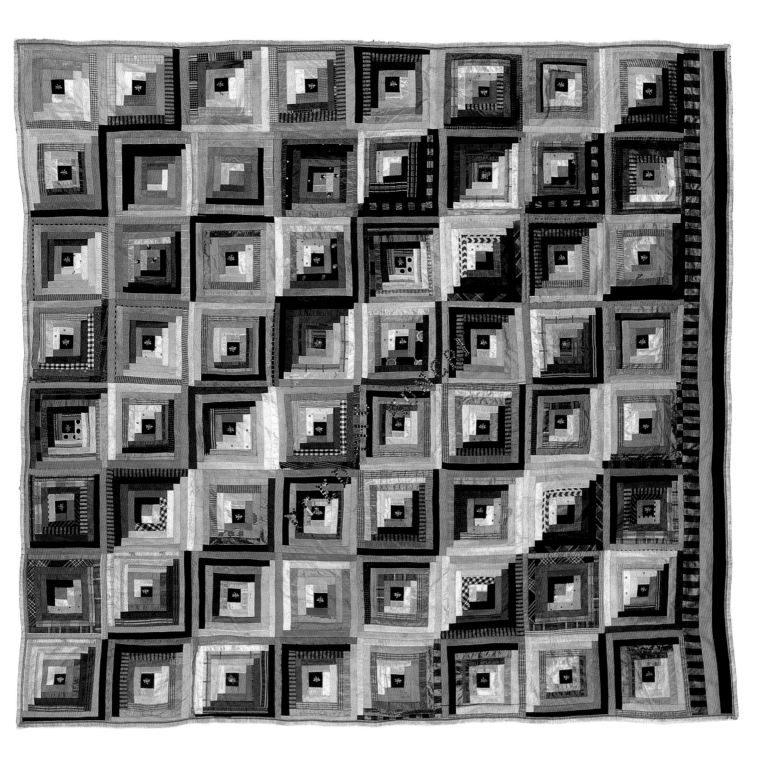

Such was the fate of many Southern households during and after the Civil War. Those who were not adversely affected by the conflict knew others who were, and the plight of those unfortunate individuals elicited sympathy and efforts to provide relief. Thus, the women of the Methodist-Episcopal Church, South in Lexington, Missouri, decided to make a quilt to auction at a church bazaar as a fundraiser for destitute Confederate families.

The minister's wife donated a black silk dress embroidered with butterflies, and other women contributed silk dresses and dressmaking scraps to use for the quilt. Each of the Log Cabin blocks was centered with one of the colorful butterflies. Someone supplied enough black-and-white-checked silk to make the back of the quilt. Someone else furnished silk ribbon to use for the binding.

The quiltmakers talked about the sadness that had come to so many families. They gave thanks when their own relatives had been spared, and they comforted their companions who had experienced loss. In their earnestness, the women wanted to leave no doubt as to the purpose of their project. They applied brass sequins diagonally across the center of the quilt to form the words "FEED THE HUNGRY." The project was a success and raised $206 for the church's relief fund.

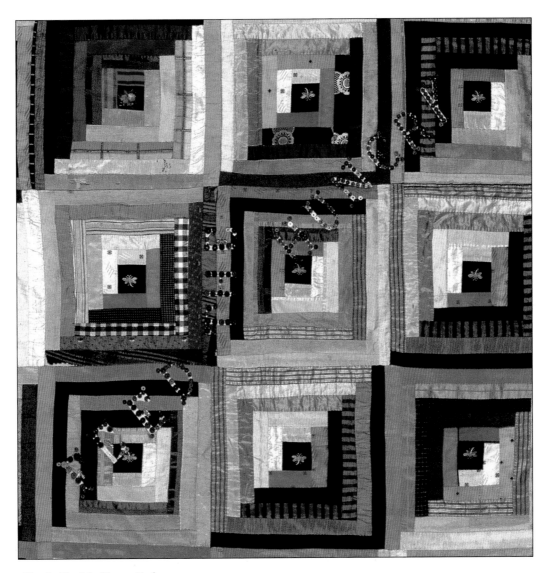

Detail of Feed the Hungry Quilt.

Lanford Album Quilt

For generations, the oral history that accompanied this Alabama album quilt stated that is was made for Lewis Lanford in 1872 in gratitude for the protection he provided the women and children of the Mount Hebron community during Reconstruction. Lost was the story of what Lewis Lanford actually did, and overlooked was the quilt's central block with the Stars and Stripes, a symbol of the "Northern aggressors."

When historian Guy Hubbs examined the quilt with Robert Cargo, his first question was how a quilt with the American flag in such a prominent position could have been made in 1872. "In Alabama," he wrote, "from the day Abraham

*The Sardis Methodist churchyard,
shown in this 1931 photograph, is
the final resting place for several of
the individuals whose names appear
on the quilt.*

Detail of Lanford Album Quilt. Initials refer to Daniel W. W. Smith (1837-1861).

Lincoln won the presidential election (November 6, 1860) until Admiral Dewey's naval victory in the Spanish-American War of 1898, no one showed the American flag with pride."

Cargo turned to the quilt itself to solve the mysteries of who made the quilt, when it was made, and why. Stylistically, the Lanford Album quilt is linked to Baltimore Album quilts, named for the city in which they originated and where, between 1845 and 1855, this type of quilt was very popular. Such quilts might have been made for a bride, a beloved minister, or a prominent citizen. Baltimore Album quilts contain blocks with floral displays in every conceivable arrangement, as well as eagles, American flags, Baltimore city monuments, ships, and trains.

Incorporating similar symbols, initialed blocks, and floral motifs in their work, the

Detail of Lanford Album Quilt. The initial inscription at left refers to Henry Lanford (1810-1883), head of the Lanford family.

Alabama women were obviously familiar with Baltimore Album quilt designs, which might have come to the community with families that migrated to the rich, fertile land of central Alabama. With its folk renderings of plants with sweet-sounding names (fire pink, flowering quince, pecan, sweet gum, and tulip poplar), this "album" provides a record of the pre-Civil War locale in which it was made.

Hubbs linked family names on the quilt—including Lanford, Powers, Bibbs, Rogers, Stephens, and Smith—to one another through census, land, and marriage records. Those persons lived in and around the community of Mount Hebron in Greene County in the mid-1800s. Of the forty-one initialed inscriptions, twenty-one were male names. Considering the large number of males from such a small community whose names appear on the quilt, it is unlikely all of them stitched their own blocks. They

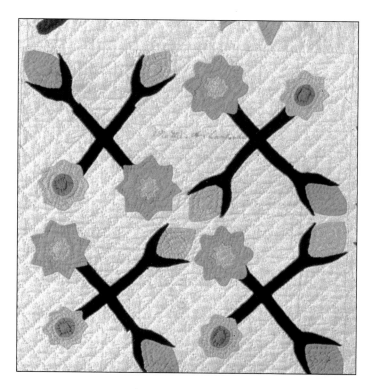

Details of Lanford Album Quilt. The inscription refers to Martha (Mattie) A. Lanford (1843-1859), daughter of Henry Lanford.

Details of Lanford Album Quilt. The motif is possibly Flowering Quince. The inscription refers to Mary E. Stevens (born 1834).

probably gave money to the project in return for someone making blocks signed with their initials.

The Sardis Methodist Church outside nearby Hopewell was the center of social activity for families in the area and the final resting place of many of the people whose names appear on the quilt. Although not yet an established fact, the quilt might have been made for a minister assigned to the church or to raise money for a church project.

Using county records, Hubbs also traced the comings, goings, and name changes of the people on the quilt. A land transaction on September 15, 1858, and a marriage on December 18, 1858, narrowed the time frame during which the quilt was made to the fall of 1858. If the quilt was made then, the mystery of the American flag would be solved, because in 1858 Abraham Lincoln had not yet been elected president, Alabama had not yet seceded from the Union, the Civil War had not yet begun, and the people of Greene County were still proudly displaying the Stars and Stripes.

"One is tempted to speculate that the American flag served to protect the quilt," wrote Robert Cargo in 1997. "Because of it, the owners may have kept the quilt out of sight, folded and stored away in a family trunk in the aftermath of the War."

Finally, what is the basis for the quilt's oral tradition, the story that Lewis Lanford had protected the town's residents during Reconstruction? Lanford's name appears on the quilt, but he was only eight years old in 1858. In 1872 he was twenty-two. Perhaps he did offer a valuable service to the people of the area during Reconstruction. Perhaps the quilt that bore the initials of so many of his family members was returned to him by a grateful family or the community itself. Perhaps it is all true. With quilts, one can only wonder.

GLOSSARY

APPLIQUÉ: laid-on pieces of cloth sewed to a background material.

BACKING: material used as the underside of a quilt.

BATT: a small unit of cotton or wool filler combed by hand or with wire brushes called cards. Also factory-made in a single sheet.

BATTING: the padding or filler of a quilt.

BINDING: finish for the raw edge of a quilt, usually done with a strip of straight-grain material in the nineteenth century.

BLOCK: a unit or section of a quilt made of joined pieces or of background material with appliquéd pieces.

BORDER: a solid, pieced, or appliquéd band at the outer edge of a quilt or surrounding a center medallion.

BRODERIE PERSE: "Persian embroidery," also known as cut-out-chintz appliqué, particularly popular prior to 1850, in which designs are cut out of glazed floral printed cotton and composed in a new arrangement on a foundation cloth.

CARDING: the act of combing cotton or wool fibers with wire brushes.

CENTER MEDALLION: an arrangement for a quilt in which one large central motif is surrounded by successive borders or other units.

COMFORT: a tied quilt.

CUT-OUT-CHINTZ APPLIQUÉ: (see Broderie Perse.)

FRAME (or quilting frame): basically four wooden poles arranged as a rectangle to which layered cloth and batting are fastened for the purpose of quilting.

LINSEY: a shortened form of linsey-woolsey, a fabric once woven of linen and wool. In the South in the nineteenth century, it was more often made of cotton and wool.

PIECED WORK: pieces joined together by seaming to make a whole, usually in geometric designs.

QUILT: two layers of cloth with padding between, stitched or tied together.

QUILTING: the act of stitching through layers of fabric and padding.

SASHING: bands added between blocks in joining.

SET: the arrangement of blocks in a quilt top design.

STUFFED WORK: quilted or appliquéd designs to which extra filler is added to create a raised surface.

TEMPLATE PIECING: a method of construction in which a fabric shape is basted to a slightly smaller paper template of the same shape and then joined to other units by whip-stitching the edges together. Frequently used with hexagonal and diamond shapes.

TOP: the upper and outer layer of a quilt.

WHITEWORK: a quilt with a top of solid white usually featuring elaborate quilting designs.

WHOLECLOTH: a quilt top made of one piece of fabric, usually three panels seamed together, and quilted.

BIBLIOGRAPHY

Adams (Henley), Bryding. "Alabama Gunboat Quilts." *Uncoverings 1987* eds. Laurel Horton and Sally Garoutte. San Francisco: American Quilt Study Group, 1989.

Adams, E. Bryding, ed. *Made in Alabama: A State Legacy*. Birmingham, AL: Birmingham Museum of Art, 1995.

Adamson, Jeremy. *Calico and Chintz: Antique Quilts from the Collection of Patricia S. Smith*. Washington, DC: Smithsonian Institution, 1997.

Allen, Gloria Seaman. *First Flowerings: Early Virginia Quilts*. Washington, DC: DAR Museum, 1987.

———— and Nancy Gibson Tuckhorn. *A Maryland Album: Quiltmaking Traditions: 1634-1934*, Nashville: Rutledge Hill Press, 1995.

Andrews, Gail C., and Janet Strain McDonald. *Black Belt to Hill Country: Alabama Quilts from the Robert and Helen Cargo Collection*. Birmingham, AL: Birmingham Museum of Art, 1982.

Arkansas Quilter's Guild. *Arkansas Quilts*. Paducah, KY: American Quilter's Society, 1987.

Atkins, Jacqueline Marx. *Shared Threads: Quilting Together Past and Present*. New York: Viking Studio Books, 1994.

Beer, Alice Baldwin. *Trade Goods: A Study of Indian Chintz in the Collection of the Cooper-Hewitt Museum*. Washington, DC: Smithsonian Institution Press, 1970.

Blankenship, Lela McDowell. *Fiddles in the Cumberlands: Letters by Amanda McDowell 1861-1865*. New York: Richard R. Smith, 1943.

Brackman, Barbara. *Clues in the Calico*. McLean, VA: EPM Publications, 1989.

————. *Quilts from the Civil War*. Lafayette, CA: C&T Publishing, 1997.

———— et al. *Material Pleasures: Quilts from the Kansas Museum of History*. Topeka, KS: Kansas State Historical Society, 1995.

———— et al. *Kansas Quilts and Quilters*. Lawrence, KS: University Press of Kansas, 1993.

Bresenhan, Karoline Patterson and Nancy O'Bryant Puentes. *Lone Stars: A Legacy of Texas Quilts, 1836-1936*, Austin, TX: University of Texas Press, 1986.

Bullard, Lacy Folmar and Betty Jo Shiell. *Chintz Quilts: Unfading Glory*. Tallahassee, FL: Serendipity Publishers, 1983.

Burdick, Nancilu B. *Legacy: The Story of Talula Gilbert Bottoms and Her Quilts*. Nashville: Rutledge Hill Press, 1988.

Campbell, Edward D. C., Jr., ed. *Before Freedom Came: African-American Life in the Antebellum South*. Charlottesville, VA: The Museum of the Confederacy and the University Press of Virginia, 1991.

Cannon, Devereaux D. Jr. *The Flags of the Confederacy: An Illustrated History*. N.p.: St. Luke's Press, 1988.

Cargo, Robert and G. Ward Hubbs. "Stitches in Time: The Lanford Album Quilt." *Alabama Heritage*, 1.1 (Summer 1986), 3-11.

Clark, Ricky. *Quilted Gardens: Floral Quilts of the Nineteenth Century*. Nashville: Rutledge Hill Press, 1994.

Clinton, Catherine. *Tara Revisited: Women and the Plantation Legend*. New York: Abbeville

Press, 1995.

Cozart, Dorothy. "The Role and Look of Fundraising Quilts 1850-1930," in Jeannette Lasansky ed. *Pieced by Mother: Symposium Papers*. Lewisburg, PA: Oral Traditions Project of the Union County Historical Society,1988.

Dunton, William Rush, Jr. *Old Quilts*. Cantonsville, MD: privately printed, 1946.

Eanes, Ellen F. "Nine Related Quilts of Mecklenburg County, 1800-1840." *Uncoverings 1982* ed. Sally Garoutte. Mill Valley, CA: American Quilt Study Group, 1983.

Faust, Drew Gilpin. *Mothers of Invention: Women of the Slaveholding South in the American Civil War*. Chapel Hill, NC: University of North Carolina Press, 1996.

Ferraro, Pat, Elaine Hedges, and Julie Silber. *Hearts and Hands: The Influence of Women and Quilts on American Society*. San Francisco: The Quilt Digest Press, 1987.

Fox, Sandi. *Wrapped in Glory: Figurative Quilts and Bedcovers 1700-1900*. Los Angeles: Los Angeles County Museum of Art, 1990.

Fox-Genovese, Elizabeth. *Within the Plantation Household: Black and White Women of the Old South*. Chapel Hill, NC: University of North Carolina Press, 1988.

Graber, John W. "One Man's Civil War." *Minnesota History*, 52.4 (Winter 1990): pp. 144-145.

Gunn, Virginia. "Quilts for Union Soldiers in the Civil War." *Uncoverings 1985* ed. Sally Garoutte, Mill Valley, CA: American Quilt Study Group, 1986.

Havig, Bettina. *Missouri Heritage Quilts*. Paducah, KY: American Quilter's Society, 1986.

Holmes, Sarah Katherine (Stone). *Brokenburn: The Journal of Kate Stone, 1861-1868* ed. John Q. Anderson, Baton Rouge, LA: Louisiana Press, 1995.

Hornback, Nancy. *Quilts in Red and Green: The Flowering of Folk Design in 19th Century America*. Wichita, KS: Wichita-Sedgwick County Historical Museum, 1992.

Horton, Laurel ed. *Quiltmaking in America: Beyond the Myths*. Nashville: Rutledge Hill Press, 1994.

———. "South Carolina Quilts in the Civil War." *Uncoverings 1985*. ed. Sally Garoutte, Mill Valley, CA: American Quilt Study Group, 1986.

——— and Lynn Robertson Myers, eds. *Social Fabric: South Carolina's Traditional Quilts*. Columbia, SC: McKissick Museum, University of South Carolina, 1985.

House, Ellen Renshaw. *A Very Violent Rebel: The Civil War Diary of Ellen Renshaw House* ed. Daniel E. Sutherland. Knoxville, TN: University of Tennessee Press, 1997

Katzenberg, Dena. *Baltimore Album Quilts*. Baltimore: The Baltimore Museum of Art, 1981.

Kentucky Quilt Project. *Kentucky Quilts 1800-1900*. Louisville: The Kentucky Quilt Project, 1982.

Kile, Michael. *The Quilt Digest 1987*. San Francisco: The Quilt Digest Press, 1987.

Kiracofe, Roderick. *The American Quilt: A History of Cloth and Comfort, 1750-1950*. New York: Clarkson Potter, 1993.

Lohrenz, Mary. "Two Lives Intertwined on a Tennessee Plantation: Textile Production as Recorded in the Diary of Narcissa L. Erwin Black." *The Southern Quarterly*, University of Southern Mississippi, Fall 1988.

——— and Anita Miller Stamper. *Mississippi Homespun: Nineteenth-Century Textiles and the Women Who Made Them*. Jackson, MS: Mississippi Department of Archives and History, 1989.

Madaus, Howard Michael. *Battle Flags of the Confederacy Army of Tennessee*. Milwaukee, WI: Milwaukee Public Museum, 1976.

Mastai, Boleslaw and Marie-Louise D'Otrange.

The Stripes and Stars: Evolution of the American Flag. Fort Worth, TX: Amon Carter Museum, 1973.

McDonald, Cornelia Peake. *A Woman's Civil War: A Diary With Reminiscences of the War from March 1862.* Madison, WI: University of Wisconsin Press, 1992.

Meriweather, Elizabeth Avery. *Recollections of 92 Years, 1824-1916.* McLean, VA: EPM Publications, 1994.

Meyer, Suellen. "The Hearth in the Home: Log Cabin Quilts in the Missouri Historical Society's Collection." *Gateway Heritage,* Missouri Historical Society, Summer, 1995.

Montgomery, Florence M. *Printed Textiles: English and American Cottons and Linens.* New York: Viking Press, 1970.

————. *Textiles in America, 1650-1870.* New York: W. W. Norton & Co., 1984.

Mounger, Kit Jeans. "Hidden Treasure." *Quilter's Newsletter Magazine.* April, 1996.

Myers, Robert Manson, ed. *The Children of Pride: A True Story of Georgia and the Civil War.* New Haven, CT: Yale University Press, 1972.

Orlofsky, Myron and Patsy. *Quilts in America.* New York: McGraw Hill Book Co., 1974. Reprint ed., New York: Abbeville Press, 1992.

Peto, Florence. *American Quilts and Coverlets.* New York: Chanticleer Press Inc, 1949.

————. *Historic Quilts.* New York: The American Historical Company, 1939.

Pettit, Florence H. *America's Printed and Painted Fabrics.* New York: Hastings House, Publishers, 1970.

Prairie Windmill Quilt History and Research Chapter, National Quilting Association. *Quilts of the Texas South Plains.* Lubbock, TX: Prairie Windmill Publishing, 1987.

Ramsey, Bets, ed. *Quilt Close-Up: Five Southern Views.* Chattanooga, TN: The Hunter Museum of Art, 1983.

————. "The Quilter," *Chattanooga Times,* 17 March 1983.

———— and Merikay Waldvogel. *Quilts of Tennessee: Images of Domestic Life Prior to 1930.* Nashville: Rutledge Hill Press, 1986.

Roberson, Ruth Haislip, ed. *North Carolina Quilts.* Chapel Hill, NC: University of North Carolina Press, 1988.

Robertson, James I., ed. *The Diary of Dolly Lunt Burge.* Athens, GA: University of Georgia Press, 1962.

Rogers Historical Museum. *Stitches in Time: A Legacy of Ozark Quilts.* Rogers, AR: Rogers Historical Museum, 1986.

Smith, Margaret Lyons. *Miss Nan Beloved Rebel,* (self-published), 1987.

Sullivan, Kathy. *Gatherings: America's Quilt Heritage.* Paducah, KY: American Quilter's Society, 1995.

Sullivan, Walter. *The War the Women Lived: Female Voices from the Confederate South.* Nashville: J. S. Sanders, 1995.

Texas Heritage Quilt Society. *Texas Quilts: Texas Treasures.* Paducah, KY: American Quilter's Society, 1986.

Trager, Judith. "Turkey Red Clues." *Quilter's Newsletter Magazine,* October 1991.

Waldvogel, Merikay. "Southern Linsey Quilts of the Nineteenth Century." *Uncoverings 1987* eds. Laurel Horton and Sally Garoutte. San Francisco: American Quilt Study Group, 1989.

Woodward, C. Vann, ed. *Mary Chesnut's Civil War.* New Haven, CT: Yale University Press, 1981.

Yabsley, Suzanne. *Texas Quilts, Texas Women.* College Station, TX: Texas A & M University Press, 1984.

Yetman, Norman R. *Life Under the "Peculiar Institution": Selections of the Slave Narrative Collection.* New York: Holt, Rinehart and Winston, 1970.

Zegart, Shelly. *American Quilt Collections: Antique Quilt Masterpieces.* Tokyo: Nihon Vogue, 1996.

CREDITS AND PERMISSIONS

Photographs are by Gary Heatherly unless otherwise noted. The antique photographs have no attribution.

A Quilter Writes About the Civil War's Causes: Excerpted from the Annie B. Darden diary in the F. Roy Johnson Collection at the North Carolina Division of Archives and History

Susan Robb Quilt: Photograph courtesy of The Museum of Texas Tech University, Lubbock.

Staying in Style: Quotations from the Emily Murrell Diary, Tennessee State Library & Archives, Nashville.

Fabric of Their Lives: Quotation from Stakeley Papers by permission of the Calvin M. McClung Historical Collection, Knox County Public Library, Knoxville, Tennessee. Quotation from Cozart-Caldwell Family papers by permission of Dorothy Cozart. Photograph of Mary High Prince Pillow courtesy of Hearts and Hands Media Arts; Sharon Risedorph, photographer.

Quilts Gone to War: Engraving courtesy of *Harper's Weekly*.

Mellichamp Quilt: Photograph courtesy of the Kansas State Historical Society, Topeka; Barry Worley, photographer.

Cherry Mansion Quilt: Quotation by permission of EPM Publications and Fort Ward Museum & Historic Site. Photograph courtesy of the Tennessee State Museum, Nashville; June Dorman, photographer.

The Poncho Quilt—Rose Tree: Engraving courtesy of *Harper's Weekly*.

Medallion Quilt: North Carolina Quilt Project. Photograph by Mark Weinkle and Greg Plachta.

Polly's Rose Quilt: Quilt photographs by Kit Jeans Mounger.

On the Home Front: Engraving courtesy of *Harper's Weekly*.

Irish Chain With Appliqué: Photograph courtesy of the Minnesota Historical Society, St. Paul; Phillip Hutchens, photographer. Engraving courtesy of *Harper's Weekly*.

Cave Hill Quilt: Quotations from *Miss Nan Beloved Rebel* by Margaret Lyons Smith, reprinted by permission of Maryanna Smith Huff. Photograph by John Edwards.

Irish Chain Flag Quilt: Quotations from *Fiddles in the Cumberlands* by Lela McDowell Blankenship (Second Edition by Jack and Betty McDowell), reprinted by permission of the family of William Jackson McDowell.

Narcissa's Quilt: Quotations by permission of *The Southern Quarterly*, 27.1 (Fall 1988): pp. 73-93. Photograph courtesy of Collection of Old Capitol Museum of Mississippi History, Jackson.

Alabama Gunboat Quilt: Quotation, Myra Inman Carter Diary, Chattanooga-Hamilton County Bicentennial Library. Photograph courtesy of the Collection of the Birmingham Museum of Art, Birmingham, Alabama. Museum purchase with partial funds from The Quilt Conservancy. Engraving courtesy of *Harper's Weekly*.

Basket Quilt: Photograph courtesy of Hearts and Hands Media Arts; Sharon Risedorph, photographer. *Surrender at Appomattox* © Tom Lovell courtesy of The Greenwich Workshop, Shelton, Connecticut. For information on the limited edition fine art prints by Tom Lovell call 1-800-243-4246.

Roses and Plumes Quilt: Courtesy of the Hunter Museum of American Art, Chattanooga, Tennessee. Engraving courtesy of *Harper's Weekly*.

Confederate Cradle Quilt: Quotation from *Mary Chesnut's Civil War*, edited by C. Vann Woodward, c. 1981, pp. 573-574, reprinted by permission of Yale University Press. Photograph courtesy of The Carter House Association, Inc., Franklin, Tennessee.

Whig's Defeat Quilt: Courtesy of the McMinn County Living Heritage Museum, Athens, Tennessee.

Hiding the Treasures: Engraving courtesy of *Harper's Weekly*.

George W. Gordon Quilt: Photograph courtesy of the Atlanta History Center, Atlanta, Georgia.

Pot of Flowers Quilt: Illustration courtesy of Tennessee State Library & Archives, Nashville.

Pieced Rose Quilt: Photograph courtesy of *The Quilts of Tennessee*; David Luttrell, photographer.

The Forest Home Quilt: Quotations from the Lucy Virginia Smith French Diary transcript, Tennessee State Library & Archives, Nashville. Photograph courtesy of the Tennessee State Museum, Nashville; June Dorman, photographer. Illustration courtesy of Tennessee State Library & Archives.

Cotton Boll Quilt: Courtesy of the North Carolina Quilt Project. Photograph by Mark Weinkle and Greg Plachta.

Cockscomb and Currant Quilt: Photograph courtesy of the Kentucky Quilt Project; David Talbott, photographer.

Commemoration: Engraving courtesy of *Harper's Weekly*.

Confederate Rose Quilt: Photograph courtesy of the Tennessee State Museum, Nashville; June Dorman, photographer.

The Blue and the Grey Log Cabin Quilt: Photograph courtesy of Judith Trager; Ken Sanville, photographer.

Reconstruction: Engraving courtesy of *Harper's Weekly*.

Rocky Mountain Quilt: Engraving courtesy of *Harper's Weekly*.

Feed the Hungry Quilt: Photograph by Bob Little, Allied Photocolor, © 1990 Missouri Historical Society.

Lanford Album Quilt: Photograph courtesy of the Birmingham Museum of Art, Birmingham, Alabama. Church photography courtesy of the William Stanley Hoole Special Collections Library, University of Alabama, Tuscaloosa.

Index